The early
British radio industry

The early British radio industry

Rowland F. Pocock

Manchester University Press
Manchester and New York

Distributed exclusively in the USA and Canada
by St. Martin's Press Inc.,
Room 400, 175 Fifth Avenue, New York, NY 10010, USA

Copyright © Rowland F. Pocock 1988

Published by Manchester University Press
Oxford Road, Manchester M13 9PL, UK

Distributed exclusively in the USA and Canada
by St. Martin's Press, Inc.,
Room 400, 175 Fifth Avenue, New York, NY 10010, USA

British Library cataloguing in publication data
Pocock, Rowland F.
  The early British radio industry
  1. Radio supplies industry—Great Britain
  —History
  I. Title
  338.4'76213841'0941   HD9696.R363G7

Library of Congress cataloging in publication data applied for

ISBN 0-7190-2621-0 *hardback*

Typeset in Great Britain
by Williams Graphics, Abergele, North Wales, UK

Printed and bound in Great Britain by
Biddles Ltd, Guildford and King's Lynn

Contents

Acknowledgements

My thanks are due to Gerald Garratt, formerly of the Science Museum, London, who first encouraged my interest in the history of radio telegraphy. I am indebted for the present work to my supervisor, Dr Jim Moore of the Open University, both for his invaluable advice and for his patience with some of my efforts. Above all, I must acknowledge the encouragement of my wife and her tolerance of the inevitable disruption of our domestic life while writing this book.

Anyone producing a study of a historical subject depends on the co-operation of numerous curators and archivists for access to essential source material. The collections which I have consulted are listed on page vii. I have met with such uniform understanding and courtesy from their staffs that it would be invidious to mention any individual by name, but I wish to record here my gratitude to all of them. However, it is only right to pay tribute to the late Betty Hance, who was archivist to The Marconi Company Limited during much of the time that I was preparing this work. Her premature death has been a loss to everyone interested in radio history.

R.F.P.

Abbreviations

Archives and manuscript collections

IEE	Institution of Electrical Engineers, Savoy Place, London WC2R 0BL
IWM	Imperial War Museum, Lambeth Road, London SE1 6HZ
MARCONI	The Marconi Company Ltd, Victoria Road, Chelmsford CM1 1NY
NAM	National Army Museum, Royal Hospital Road, London SW3 4HT
NHL	Naval Historical Library, Empress State Building, London SW6 1TR
NMM	National Maritime Museum, Greenwich, London SE10 9NF
PO	Post Office Records, St Martins le Grand, London EC1A 1PG
PRO	Public Record Office, Chancery Lane, London WC2A 1LR
RNLI	Royal National Lifeboat Institution, Poole BH15 1HZ
SCI MUS	Science Museum, South Kensington, London SW7 2DD

Journals

Inst PO Electr. Eng. J.	*Institute of Post Office Electrical Engineers Journal*
J Franklin Inst.	*Journal of the Franklin Institute*
J Soc. Teleg. Eng.	*Journal of the Society of Telegraph Engineers*
Life-Boat J.	*Life-Boat Journal*
Naval Eng. J.	*Naval Engineers' Journal*

Philos. Mag.	*Philosophical Magazine*
Philos. Trans. R. Soc.	*Philosophical Transactions of the Royal Society*
Proc. Inst. Electr. Eng.	*Proceedings of the Institution of Electrical Engineers*
Proc. R. Inst.	*Proceedings of the Royal Institution*
Proc. R. Soc.	*Proceedings of the Royal Society*
Prof. Papers C. R. Eng.	*Professional Papers of the Corps of Royal Engineers*
Rep. Brit. Assoc.	*Report of the British Association for the Advancement of Science*
Sci. Amer.	*Scientific American*
Sci. Trans. R. Dublin Soc.	*Scientific Transactions of the Royal Dublin Society*

Introduction

An industry in the ascendant?

The invisible electromagnetic radiation which is the basis of radio telegraphy was discovered in 1887 by Heinrich Hertz (1857–94), Professor of Physics at Karlsruhe Polytechnic. His discovery was discussed at the next annual meeting of the British Association. The distinguished Irish mathematician George Fitzgerald (1857–1901) then declared triumphantly that in consequence humanity had 'won the battle lost by the giants of old [and] snatched the thunderbolt from Jove himself'.[1] Within a relatively short time, Fitzgerald saw the partial justification of this optimistic claim. In the summer of 1898, while a passenger in a launch chartered by the *Dublin Daily Express*, he witnessed the world's first radio press dispatch. After a decade, 'Hertzian' waves were no longer the concern only of pure physics. They were being put to use in a practical communications industry.

Landes's study of the industrialisation of Western Europe describes this radio industry which evolved between 1887 and 1898 as typical of modern enterprises based on advanced scientific principles. He claims that most of the characteristics of recent technological progress can be identified in the radio industry. In particular, Landes notes the international researches in pure and applied science which contributed to its development, pointing out that

The array of scientists and technicians who shared in the early development of the wireless reads like a UNESCO committee: Oliver Lodge and J. A. Fleming in England; Edouard Branly in France; Alexander Popov in Russia; Guglielmo Marconi in Italy and then England; Ferdinand Braun, Rudolf Slaby and Georg von Arco in Germany; Reginald Fessenden and Lee De Forest in the United States.[2]

The first radio company as such was the Wireless Telegraph and Signal Company Ltd, registered in London on 20 July 1897. It was founded specifically to market the patents of Guglielmo Marconi (1874–1937). An Italian national, but with a British mother, Marconi was as well known in Britain as in his native country. This first company was soon confronted by a number of competitors. Eugene Ducretet (1844–1908), a Parisian scientific-instrument maker, started manufacturing radio sets a few months after the foundation of Marconi's company. Slaby and von Arco formed a radio department within the German electrical giant AEG during 1898. Braun established a second German radio company, with the Siemens and Halske group as principal shareholders, in the following year. The international scientific contribution to radio, identified by Landes, was soon matched by an international movement for its commercial exploitation. Germany's large electrical manufacturers were prominent in this movement. By the beginning of the twentieth century, there were indigenous radio companies in Britain, France, Germany and Italy – and a State-owned radio workshop for the Russian Navy.

Britain's dominance of the world's radio industry

The foregoing description outlines the development of radio merely by reiterating details already published in other studies. Landes's book is singled out for quotation only as a typical example of many general industrial histories. To this extent, the narrative so far may be called the accepted history of radio. But the present work departs from 'accepted' history at this point. For there are, in fact, important aspects of radio development which do not conform with these general histories of industry. Other nineteenth-century technologies, it is true, originated like radio in Britain and were later developed abroad. Other British companies were, like the radio industry, founded by foreign entrepreneurs. But these events are usually presented as part of Britain's industrial decline. The growth of foreign, and especially German, industry at the expense of Britain is a familiar theme. And yet this decline was not universal, and the radio industry is an important exception to the general pattern.

For Britain's radio industry dominated the world's market until the First World War. Previous studies of radio's origins have concentrated on technological developments and so ignored this commercial paradox. But the present work considers the industry's social and economic aspects, and does not just catalogue its technical achievements. It cannot therefore adopt the viewpoint categorised here as 'accepted' history. The fact of dominance, and not of decline, has to be its starting-point. And so it must identify the causes of this dominance within the very same society which other historians have shown to contain the causes of decline. But it must start by re-stating briefly the general facts of the country's industrial failings and establishing that radio was indeed an exception.

Britain's economic decline is the subject of several modern studies. However, its symptoms were identifed by Lyon Playfair (1818–98) as early as 1867. He was then particularly concerned with Germany's technological progress, as evident in comparison with Britain's display at the Paris exhibition. By the end of the nineteenth century the effects of the decline were evident. Germany was by then producing nearly as much sulphuric acid as Britain, and considerably more pig-iron. These two particular indicators might be ascribed simply to the appearance of rivals in traditional British markets. But the weakness of British industry in the face of German competition was then even more apparent in the newer advanced technologies. Germany's manufacturers produced twice the output (by value) of Britain's heavy electrical industry and ninety per cent of the world's synthetic dyes. Similar comparisons could be made for many of the new industries which were founded during the recovery from the 1873–95 depression. Aviation, automobiles and other applications of the internal combustion engine, the adoption of mass-production techniques, the introduction of technology into the domestic economy with such items as the sewing machine, all owed more to foreign than to British enterprise during the late nineteenth century. It seemed as if, in Hobsbawm's words, 'Britain failed to adapt to new conditions, not because she could not, but because she did not wish to.'[3]

In contrast, the balance of the international radio market was very much in Britain's favour. The success of the British radio industry, in comparison with other manufacturers, is the more remarkable for being in an advanced technology. It was also remarkable for being achieved in the face of strong German competition. For AEG merged its radio interests with Siemens and Halske to form the single Telefunken organisation in 1903. Such mergers into 'cartels' were a familiar feature of successful German industries, and Telefunken enjoyed many of the advantages of a cartel. They had access to the manufacturing and sales expertise of their parent companies. Moreover, they were financed by the Deutsche Bank, who, as investors in the Norddeutscher Lloyd shipping company, had useful sales contacts.[4] And yet the Marconi group, without powerful electrical manufacturers or bankers to support them, retained a leading place in the world's industry.

Contemporary estimates, sometimes based, it is true, on German publicity material, suggested that Telefunken's sales exceeded those of Marconi between 1903 and 1905.[5] But by 1912 there were 953 Marconi radio sets operating world-wide, against only 478 supplied by the German company. The success of the Marconi operation is even more marked if only those countries outside the British and German Empires are considered. In these nations, where the companies presumably were competing on more or less equal terms, Marconi had supplied 322 sets, while only 114 were from Telefunken.[6] Marconi concluded an advantageous agreement with Telefunken at about this time, defining their mutual spheres of interest.

It was also in 1912 that a Marconi subsidiary took over several rivals to become America's largest radio company.[7] Britain thus advanced to dominate the world's radio industry during the years before the First World War.

How could one British company do so well at a time and place when many others were failing? This thesis advances an explanation consistent with the well-documented general decline of the country's other industries during the late nineteenth century.

Industrial decline and the growth of empire

There is no shortage of explanations for Britain's industrial decline during the last quarter of the nineteenth century. Wiener's recent analysis of national economics and culture describes this decline as 'the leading problem of modern British history'.[8] Certainly several modern historical studies have been devoted to this particular theme. Some of these studies emphasise the disadvantages experienced in the 1870s as a consequence of having been the first industrialised nation. Companies used traditional processes that could not be adapted to utilise new supplies of raw materials. Industries could not raise new capital to replace old machinery with more efficient modern plant. Conservative industrialists saw no need to change traditional practices that had served them well for half a century or more. According to this explanation of industrial decline, innovative industries should be less burdened with traditional techniques and obsolescent plant than their predecessors. New technologies may flourish in the same society in which older technologies are becoming moribund. Sturmey's history considers radio as an innovative industry. It does not, however, point up the interesting contrast between the radio industry's success and the country's unhappy experience with other innovative industries like organic chemicals and heavy electrical engineering.[9]

Wiener suggests that the decline was due to sociological rather than economic causes.[10] He considers that modern British culture is fundamentally anti-industrial. It has been, he suggests, strongly influenced by a 'rural myth' about an idealised community based on small-scale agriculture and craft workshops. In practice, the wealthiest industrialists and merchants have often been those who have made their money from large-scale technology. But such individuals are expected to abandon their wealth-making vocations in order to be admitted into the ranks of the gentry. The educational system reflects this distinction, encouraging the study of arts, classics and pure science rather than applied science and technology. Lyon Playfair, who, in 1867, criticised Britain's failure to exploit new technologies, believed that Germany's success resulted from that nation's encouragement of scientific and technical education.

It was certainly true that Britain's provision for scientific training was less than in the country's principal rivals. For instance, as Corelli Barnett has shown, in 1900 Germany had five times as many students in technical colleges and universities as Britain – and spent twenty times as much in university grants.[11] Randman points out that the National Physical Laboratory, founded in 1898, received less than a tenth of the initial grant and only about a quarter of the annual budget of comparable institutions in the USA and Germany.[12] In the early part of the nineteenth century, graduates of the Continental universities often came to Britain seeking work in industry. By the second half of the century, however, as Cardwell observes: 'the immigrants were no longer employees; they had become employers, entrepreneurs and pioneers of the new science-based industries. In this important group we find such people as Ludwig Mond, Charles Dreyfus, Hans Renold, William Siemens, Heinrich Simon, and Guglielmo Marconi'.[13] But, here again, the radio industry does not conform with the general rule. Marconi had not received a university education. His scientific knowledge was no better than that available to most young Englishmen of the time.

The most common explanations of decline may therefore be classed as economic, emphasising industry's problems with innovation (and the necessary capitalisation), or social, drawing attention to the deficiencies of the educational system. Neither explanation accounts in itself for the radio industry's success. Playfair's contemporary, Karl Marx (1818–1883), integrated economic and social causes in a single explanation. According to Marx, the decline of Britain's industries was an inherent and inevitable consequence of a capitalist economy. As those nations which were formerly dependent on Britain's exports (notably in Europe and the USA) had industrialised, so, he said, the total production of world industry had expanded beyond the size of the available market.

But Marx's explanation introduced another factor which could account for the paradoxical success of certain industries. The capitalists' solution was to absorb their excess production '… by the conquest of new markets, and by the more thorough exploitation of the old ones'.[14] British trade shifted away from the industrialised nations to the less-developed territories of the Empire during the last quarter of the nineteenth century. Trade depended on communications. Submarine cable telegraphs provided a reliable means of exchanging information and transmitting instructions from central government and business offices to the overseas dependencies. Steamships supplied a comparable (albeit slower) service for goods and personnel. Radio telegraphy supplemented these two existing systems, allowing for communication from ship to ship and from ship to cable terminal on shore. The existence of the Empire was an essential modifying factor in the nation's social and economic systems. It created a need for radio technology and a market for the products of the radio industry.

By 1900, there were radio industries in five countries – Britain, France, Germany, Italy and Russia. It is no coincidence that these five were the major colonising powers during the nineteenth century. For the purposes of this study, the growths of these European empires may be divided into three fairly distinct periods. The first period covers the years up to about 1870, when the empires were limited to existing colonies. After 1870, the second period of developing Imperialism was one largely of expansion from these existing frontiers. There was what amounts to a formal start to this period in Britain, when Disraeli – who twenty years earlier had described 'these wretched colonies' as 'a millstone round our necks' – was returned to power at the 1874 election on a programme committed to Imperialist policies. Italy, too, made a formal start to its colonial expansion. In 1869, the Congress of Chambers of Commerce at Genoa asked their government to establish a trading station on the Red Sea; the government purchased the port of Assab, which remained for many years Italy's sole overseas possession. France began to advance from the African colonies in Algeria, Senegal and Somalia in 1872, while Russia, following the Treaty of Aigun, started military operations in Central Asia during 1864. Britain was not the first to initiate this phase of colonialism, and it was France who acquired the most territory.

The third and final period of expansion of the great European empires is also the period of this study of the origins of the radio industry — the two final decades of the nineteenth century. Germany, newly unified in Europe, joined the scramble for colonies by establishing garrisons in Africa and the Pacific. France consolidated its territories in Africa and Indo-China. Russia continued to advance along the Chinese borders towards Manchuria and Korea. Italian armies moved out from Assab to occupy the whole of Eritrea. The largest territorial gains of this period were, however, made by Britain in Southern and Western Africa. These advances could sometimes result in meetings and near-conflict, as, for example, in the confrontation of British and French troops at Fashoda on the Upper Nile in 1898. Such meetings were eventually averted by mutual agreement between the European powers to create what Hobsbawm has called 'informal empires'[15] of agreed spheres of influence among the under-developed independent nations. France was allowed to trade without competition in parts of Central Africa and the Pacific, Italy enjoyed similar privileges in Tripolitania, and Britain with the republics of South America.

This last phase of colonial expansion ended with a series of military reverses for the European powers. An Italian army was defeated by the Abyssinians at Adowa in 1896; Britain encountered unexpectedly strong resistance from the Boer republics in 1899–1902; Russia's advance through Asia was finally halted by Japanese troops in Korea during 1904–5.

All of these empires, save one, were composed of overseas colonies. The single exception, the Russian Empire, was confined to the Eurasian land mass and was contiguous with European Russia. Nevertheless, its coastline of nearly 50,000 kilometres was two-and-a-half times as long as its land frontiers. Russia needed railways and line telegraphs to communicate across and unite this giant territory, just as the overseas empires needed steamships and submarine cables.

And all of the empires needed navies to protect their merchant shipping and their shores, as well as to escort the transports which carried their armies to foreign conquests.

Imperial navies as markets for the radio industry

It was in fact the navies and not the overseas colonies themselves which provided the best markets for the early radio companies. Great Britain, France and Russia all built up large fleets of modern warships in the 1880s and 1890s. Italy, too, engaged in this naval arms race, but ambition outran resources late in the century. The four most powerful European navies during the period of this study were, therefore, those of the four nations which started Imperial expansion in about 1870. The fifth of the Imperial powers, Germany, did not join the struggle for colonies until 1884. Likewise the build-up of the modern German fleet started at the very end of the nineteenth century. Naval expansion was eventually accepted in most industrial countries as an essential feature of Imperialist political policy – especially after the publication of Mahan's *The Influence of Sea Power on History* in 1890.

Large navies needed an efficient means of ship-to-ship communication. Admirals, especially, needed some means of sending orders to the scattered vessels under their command. The battlefleets of the Imperial powers were valued customers of the nascent radio industry. The Wireless Telegraph and Signal Company, founded in 1897, was particularly favoured as the Royal Navy was then the largest in the world. Three of the Royal Navy's first-line warships were fitted with Marconi radio sets for manoeuvres in July 1899. The performance of this equipment persuaded the Admiralty to equip a large proportion of the fleet with radio apparatus. The newly-created German fleet (as well as the expanding non-European fleets of the USA and Japan) was less ready to use this new signalling system. Indeed, the Germany navy accepted a few sets in 1902 only after considerable pressure from the Kaiser himself. It was rumoured at the time that the vital decision was taken when Grand-Admiral Tirpitz, the Navy Minister, was temporarily off duty. The German radio enthusiasts were able to concentrate their efforts on a less forceful deputy! Imperial communications and Imperial defence together favoured the development of Britain's radio industry, despite the country's failure to exploit other technologies. Their

German rivals, supplying a smaller and less technologically – conscious fleet, lacked this advantage.

The radio industry may not be entirely typical of those which Marx described as seeking new markets in the colonies. But it undoubtedly found its best customer in the navy which protected trade with and between these colonies. And the relationship between the industry and this important customer influenced both the commercial and the technical development of radio. Earlier histories of radio have not recognised the great importance of this market. They have not, in consequence, identified the contrast between the successful innovation of radio with the co-operation of an agency of Imperial government, and those less successful innovative enterprises which did not enjoy such support. Most existing histories, in fact, suppose that such government support as there was came from the Post Office telegraphs. Even Sturmey's otherwise excellent study overestimates the contribution of the Post Office and its engineer-in-chief, William Preece (1834–1913) to radio development.[16] In fact, the Post Office's contribution during the industry's early years was negligible. With the public records of the period now available, the present work at last puts the record straight in this respect.

Imperial influences on applied science

Part of the British radio industry's success can therefore be ascribed to Imperial policies which provided a market for its products. It was encouraged to introduce new technology, while other industries with only domestic markets had less incentive to innovate. But Imperialism had social as well as economic consequences. Wiener's 'rural myth' may have inhibited the teaching of science in most of the country's schools and universities. Imperialism was a counter influence. At least some of those responsible for Imperial communications and defence received a sound education in applied science.

During most of the period of this study, from 1885 to 1905, the Empire was governed by a Unionist coalition of reformist elements from the Liberal and Conservative parties. They continued existing trends to increased centralisation of authority. Programmes of social reform by preceding Liberal and Conservative administrations extended State control into many areas of domestic politics. Reform of the Army, of the Civil Service, the introduction of State primary

schools, the improvement of public health through various Factory
Acts and Pure Food Acts, had created a corps of government teachers,
inspectors and examiners to replace the heterogenous collection of
representatives from the Church and other charitable agencies who
had previously provided these services. The Unionist administration
continued this process of rationalisation and centralisation by creating
a hierarchy of local and municipal councils to administer the growing
number of public services. It extended the concept of centralised
authority into foreign policy with proposals for greater unity of the
Empire through the federation of colonial administrations and by the
adoption of a single Imperial economic system.

Cardwell's study of British science at this period suggests that
Imperialist policies were one cause of the nation's industrial decline.
He states that the attempt to

establish dominion over countless square miles of jungle, desert and swamp
was surely to mistake the outward appearances of power for its essential inner
structure. How effective all this was in diverting the energy and ambitions
of able young men from the pursuits of technology, industry and perhaps
even of science can only be conjectured, for the roots of Imperial ambition
must have reached far back into the public schools where so many of the
nation's middle-class youth were being educated. How many young men from
such schools would seriously have considered a career with, for example,
Beyer-Peacock or Brunner-Mond?[17]

But the individual 'Imperial ambition' criticised by Cardwell could
often be fulfilled within the established communications industries
which helped to maintain the Empire. Lieutenant Chard, for example,
was an officer of Royal Engineers employed on such duties. But he
became a national hero during the Zulu War of 1879 when awarded
the Victoria Cross for his conduct of the defence of Rorke's Drift.

Imperialist policies encouraged the centralisation of authority and
depended on the products of science-based industries. They led
logically to the provision of a centralised State-controlled scientific
education system. Writers in reformist journals like the *Fortnightly
Review*, the *Pall Mall Gazette*, and *The Times* had supported such
a system for many years before 1880. Gladstone's administrations
of 1886 and 1892–95 have been described as 'firmly opposed' to the
State support of science.[18] The leaders of the Imperially-minded
Unionist cabinet were more sympathetic. In addition to their general
commitment to social reform, they were unusually well-informed
about contemporary science and technology.[19] They responded

positively to demands for more investment in scientific education. Acts of 1889 and 1890 encouraged municipal authorities to invest public and charitable funds in technical colleges. A direct government grant of £15,000 a year was approved in 1888 for the provincial University Colleges in such industrial centres as Liverpool, Manchester and Bristol. The existing grant to the University of London (then merely an examining body which served to co-ordinate the syllabuses of an otherwise miscellaneous collection of teaching institutions) was increased, while a Royal Commission considered how best to reconstitute the University in order to improve facilities for studying science in the Capital. As a more immediate measure to stimulate scientific research at the highest levels, the remaining funds of the Commissioners for the 1851 Exhibition were allocated to the provision of Exhibition Fellowships at the leading universities.

The amount of money invested in these schemes for the State support of science was small by contemporary German and American standards. All the same, it was a considerable increase over the funding provided by previous governments. It was clear evidence of official recognition of the importance of science to the Empire.

The provision for scientific training within the State education system was therefore increasing as the Empire expanded. But the most direct and obvious contribution of scientific education to Imperial communications and defence was made by the military academies. In fact, the Army had been providing a technical education for artillery and engineer officers at the Royal Military College, Woolwich, since 1801. Royal Engineer officers were employed as school inspectors for science subjects during the early years of the State education system, and assisted in the repair and extension of the national telegraph network after its nationalisation in 1870. The Royal Navy's technical education system – which was particularly significant in the development of radio telegraphy – started somewhat later, in 1859. A young man intending to follow a naval career entered *HMS Britannia*, the Royal Naval College at Dartmouth, at the age of thirteen. He there received two years of classroom training followed by one year at sea in a training ship. Then, rated as Midshipman, he was posted to one of the ships of the Fleet for a further three years of training by professional instructors. He could then sit the examination for Lieutenant and, having passed the examination, achieve the status of a commissioned officer.[20] Within a few years he would be expected to return to full-time study at the Royal Naval

College, Greenwich for instruction, as appropriate to his special-
isation, in such topics as thermodynamics, mechanics, materials and
structures, navigation and meterology.[21] Even then, he would not
have completed his scientific education. Ambitious officers expected
to attend further courses of advanced technical study, such as ballistics
at the gunnery school, HMS *Excellent*, or electrical engineering at the
torpedo school, HMS *Vernon*.

The naval officer therefore started his professional education at
the age when his civilian contemporaries would have been entering
the public schools. A committee of educationalists monitoring the
cadets' progress through the Royal Naval College in the 1870s found
that standards were high in comparison with the best civilian schools,
but criticised the lack of a 'general education'.[22] This was almost
certainly a reference to the total absence of classics from the curricu-
lum, and a corresponding emphasis on technical subjects – of thirty-
two and a half hours each week spent in the classroom, seventeen were
devoted to mathematics and related topics. As a result *all* naval
officers received some higher education in applied science. The Royal
Navy's prejudices might still emphasise the values of discipline and
smartness, rather than engineering. But at least there was no overt
stigma associated with the study of 'useful' subjects. Henry Jackson
(1855–1929), a torpedo officer who would become one of the
country's leading radio engineers and the first Chairman of the Radio
Research Board, eventually achieved the rank of Admiral of the Fleet
and was appointed First Sea Lord. John Fisher (1841–1920), a
gunnery specialist, who as First Sea Lord was responsible for a major
programme of naval modernisation and reform, was a respected
adviser of the government and confidant of King Edward VII. Prince
George (1865–1936, later King George V), second in line to the
throne, entered HMS *Britannia* in 1877 and completed the electrical
engineering course at HMS *Vernon* in 1885. Wiener comments that
a civilian 'gentleman' could not study engineering and was not
expected to follow a career in industry. But even Royalty might study
engineering in order to become a naval officer and defend the Empire.

Britain's radio industry benefited considerably from the existence
of the Empire. The overseas colonies needed efficient communications, of which radio telegraphy was a part. A large navy, to defend
these colonies and their communications, was a valuable ready-made
market for a marine wireless telegraphy system – especially when
the senior officers of that navy were trained engineers who could

assess the merits of contemporary technologies. And the Imperial government's education policy ensured that there were enough applied scientists to meet the needs of this industry, even if State investment in applied science were inadequate by Continental standards. These three factors are considered in more detail in the body of this work; Part 1 describes the Empire's systems of maritime communications and the ways in which both the Royal Navy and the merchant marine came to recognise their needs for an efficient wireless telegraph; Part 2 analyses the contributions of the applied scientists and engineers who developed radio from a laboratory apparatus into a useful communications system, and shows that the more significant of these contributions came from scientists who had been educated within the State's system; Part 3 shows that the contribution of the Post Office to radio development during the nineteenth century was negligible, (despite the impression conveyed by other histories of radio) and explains how, instead, the new system of radio telegraphy was adopted to meet the Empire-wide communications needs of the Royal Navy.

References

1 *The Times*, 8 September 1888.
2 D.S. Landes, *The Unbound Prometheus*, Cambridge, Cambridge University Press [1969] 1980, pp. 424–5.
3 E.J. Hobsbawm, *Industry and Empire*, Harmondsworth, Penguin, 1969, p. 182.
4 C. Trebilcock, *The Industrialization of the Continental Powers*, London, Longman, 1981, p. 70.
5 For example, the *Annual Report of the Torpedo School (HMS Vernon)*, for 1904, p. 12 (NHL) suggests that Telefunken had supplied as many radio installations as all other manufacturers together.
6 H. Pieper, 'Die englischen Bemühungen vor dem Ersten Weltkrieg um ein Weltweites Kabel-und Funkmonopol', *Archiv Für deutsche Postgeschichte*, I, 1975, p. 95.
7 G.L. Archer, *History of Radio to 1926*, New York, American Historical Society, 1938, p. 101.
8 M.J. Weiner, *English Culture and the Decline of the Industrial Spirit*, Cambridge, Cambridge University Press, 1981, p. 3.
9 S.G. Sturmey, *The Economic Development of Radio*, London, Duckworth, 1958.
10 Wiener, *English Culture*, pp. 132–7.
11 C. Barnett, 'Technology, education and industrial and economic strength', *Journal of the Royal Society of Arts*, CXXVII, 1979, pp. 118–27.
12 P. Randman, *Government Science in Britain, 1875–1921*, MSc Thesis, University of Manchester, 1977, pp. 78–80.

13   D. S. L. Cardwell, *The Organisation of Science in England*, London, Heinemann, 1972, p. 188.

14   K. Marx and F. Engels, *The Communist Manifesto*, Harmondsworth, Penguin [1888] 1978, p. 86.

15   Hobsbawm, *Industry and Empire*, p. 150.

16   Sturmey, *Development of Radio*, pp. 15–31.

17   Cardwell, *Science in England*, p. 191.

18   Randman, *Government Science*, p. 26.

19   Chamberlain worked in his family's engineering business before entering politics; Lord Salisbury, an amateur botanist and chemist of some repute, was President of the British Association in 1894; Balfour was a Fellow of the Royal Society and President of the British Association in 1904.

20   'Report of the Committee on the Higher Education of Naval Officers', 1870, p. ix (NHL).

21   'Report of the Committee Appointed to Inquire into the Establishment of the Royal Naval College, Greenwich', 1877, pp. 83–4 (NHL).

22   'Report of the Committee Appointed by the Admiralty to Inquire into the System of Training Naval Cadets on board HMS *Britannia*', 1875 (NHL).

PART I

Centralisation and communications

Chart of principal events, 1883–1896

	Royal Navy	Coastal Rescue Services	General Post Office
1883		Re-organisation of RNLI	State takes control of telephone system
1884			
1885		Cable failures emphasise problem of communication with lightships	
1886			
1887	Torpedo boat communication problem discovered during trials in Mediterranean		Preece's dispute with Heaviside about telephone transmission lines
1888	Communications problems confirmed during Fleet's annual manoeuvres		Preece's dispute with Lodge about lightning conductors
1889			
1890		RNLI sets up sub-committee to consider offshore telegraphs	

1891		Trotter's suggestion of radio in *The Electrician*	Inductive telegraph trials at Lavernock
1892	Further trials emphasise the torpedo boat communications problem	Royal Commission set up to investigate coastal communications	Preece appointed engineer-in-chief
1893	Loss of HMS *Victoria* Increase in Navy Estimates		
1894	HMS *Vernon* instructed to investigate torpedo boat communications		Inductive telegraph trials at Loch Ness
1895	Line telegraphs tested between ships at anchor		
1896			Inductive telegraph fails during tests at Dover

1

Imperial requirements

... communication of government orders ... to all parts of the
Empire ...   J. and J. W. Brett, 1845

The first radio company in Britain, and indeed the first in the world,
was founded in 1897. Until then, submarine cables were the only
available commercial means of electric telegraphy beyond the
coastline. For twenty-five years before the introduction of radio, a
time of Imperial expansion, these cables maintained vital links with
the overseas colonies. Civil servants in Whitehall depended on the
cable network for communication with colonial administrators. But,
although the inland telegraphs had been nationalised in 1870, the cable
companies remained in private hands. They were organised to provide
an adequate service which gave priority to government messages.
There were few demands for public ownership.

This organisation was due to the efforts of Sir John Pender
(1816–96), founder of the Anglo-American company which financed
the first successful transatlantic cable. Between 1870 and 1880
he negotiated agreements providing further transatlantic lines
and connections from Britain to the Far East and Australasia. The
cables of his Eastern Telegraph Company were routed through the
Mediterranean and Aden to India. Another of his companies, the
Eastern Extension, continued the service to South-East Asia, China
and Australia. Only two important companies – linking Britain with
Scandinavia and Russia, and carrying South American traffic –
remained outside the Pender group by 1877. Neither of these companies, it will be noted, handled essential Imperial communications.

During the final quarter of the nineteenth century, the submarine
cable industry developed a structure similar to that of Germany's
successful cartels. The methods by which competing companies were
united differed somewhat, but the ultimate sanction was economic
in both countries. Pender, with his important financial and political
contacts, played much the same role in the British cable companies

as did investment banks in the German electrical, chemical and steel industries. In the manner of a cartel, Pender's group controlled investment and prices to bring the best return and discourage potential rivals. Charges were reduced gradually as the cable network expanded. Tariffs were always set high enough to keep normal demands well below the cables' maximum capacity (thereby keeping adequate reserve for peak loadings and long-term increases in traffic), yet sufficiently low to persuade foreign businessmen that it would not be worth investing in competing cables of their own.[1]

Radio telegraphy was developed at a time, therefore, when Britain was already establishing a successful industry for electrical communications. The scale of that success is illustrated by the statistics in Table 1.1. Pender and other British entrepreneurs owned most of the world's cables during the last quarter of the nineteenth century.

Table 1.1 *Submarine Cables owned (km)*
(% of world total in brackets)

	1872	1894	1900
Britain	42,740 (77·7%)	192,800 (65·8%)	240,690 (67·8%)
USA	–	46,880 (16·0%)	39,410 (11·1%)
France	6,325 (11·5%)	16,995 (5·8%)	35,806 (10·1%)
Denmark	5,940 (10·8%)	12,600 (4·3%)	14,560 (4·1%)
Germany	–	4,102 (1·4%)	6,390 (1·8%)
Others	–	19,630 (6·7%)	18,100 (5·1%)

Source: Pieper, Die englischen Bemühungen, p. 95.

It was a period when other British industries were losing their traditional markets to German and American competitors. Yet the submarine cable companies achieved and consolidated a position of world dominance. This achievement was particularly unusual with an advanced technology like electric telegraphy. It contrasted with the nation's poor commercial showing against foreign competition in other advanced technologies like chemistry and electric power.

Science and State support for submarine cables

These results appear to contradict Lyon Playfair and his colleagues who, during the 1870s and 1880s, complained of Britain's industrial failings. But these critics may well have considered the submarine cable industry's successes vindicated their views. They believed that most British businesses paid too little attention to science. And, exceptionally, the cable companies employed scientific consultants from their earliest years. In fact, some of the first successful experiments with submarine telegraphs had been carried out by the physicist Charles Wheatstone (1802–75) at Swansea Bay in 1844. The formal or informal partnership of a physicist with an engineer/business man became a common feature of the telegraph and cable companies. Michael Faraday was consulted by Latimer Clark, chief engineer of the Electric Telegraph Company in its early days. Lord Kelvin[2] assisted Charles Bright (who supervised the laying of the first successful Atlantic cables) and Fleeming Jenkin. John Muirhead, a manufacturer of telegraphic instruments, employed his son, Alexander (a DSc of London University) as scientific advisor. This practice was continued later in the radio industry, Marconi retaining Erskine-Murray, Fleming and Lodge at various times as scientific consultants. When the German-born engineer William Siemens observed in 1876 that 'Submarine cables are specifically British enterprises. I might go further and say every submarine cable which is now working is almost without exception the produce of this country, and has been shipped from the Thames',[3] he was paying tribute to Britain's physicists as well as the country's manfacturers.

But the cables companies' impressive commercial record was not due solely to their recognition of the importance of science. These companies enjoyed an unusual level of government support, which also contributed to their success. The relationship between communications and government was emphasised in the earliest proposal for a submarine cable from Britain. The brothers John Watkins Brett (1805–63) and Jacob Brett (1808–98) then suggested to the Prime Minister that

The advance and power offered to the Government by this invention render it of the greatest importance that they should have it under their own control ... the following are a few of the advantages offered by this patent ... immediate communication of government orders and dispatches to all part of the Empire, and the instant return of answers to the same from the seats of local government.[4]

Despite this recital of expected benefits, the government offered neither to finance the project nor to purchase the patents. The Bretts eventually laid their first cable to France as a private venture in 1850.

After 1870, with Imperial responsibilities increasing, the government took more account of this new means of communication. Their encouragement was not always obvious, but it was nevertheless significant. Even the continued existence of the Pender group of companies was itself a token of government approval. The Unionist administration in office during the last two decades of the nineteenth century favoured centralised control of public services. But they did not extend this policy so far as to approve of private monopolies. Indeed, the Electric Lighting Act of 1882 was intended to discourage their development in the electricity supply industry. Monopoly was tolerated among the submarine cable companies while it served the government's purposes. In return for various subsidies, the companies gave government business priority over all other traffic. Imperial communications had security comparable with that guaranteed to official inland communications over the Post Office telegraph lines, but without the political complication of outright nationalisation. This semi-official monopoly was satisfactory while official dispatches were transmitted over routes where commercial traffic covered the expenses.

Pender's monopoly remained largely unchallenged until after his death. Until then, government intervention was confined to the operation of relatively short lines and the payment of compensation when companies re-routed cables for non-commercial reasons. But in 1897 a Colonial Office committee recommended the construction of a government-owned cable across the Pacific. It was unlikely that a private company could recover the costs of such an undertaking from the business traffic. Nevertheless, the Eastern Telegraph Company objected and offered instead to provide a second cable via the Cape of Good Hope to Australia.[5] In spite of this offer, the Pacific cable project went ahead. Financed jointly by the governments of Britain, Canada, Australia and New Zealand, it went into service in 1902.

Experience had shown that an Imperial government needed communications. Peel's ministry had not recognised this need when they rejected the Bretts' request for financial assistance in 1850. But that had been before the adoption of avowedly Imperialist political policies. Some fifty years later, government involvement was not confined even to the provision of subsidies for the cable companies.

While existing routes were left to private enterprise, new cables of doubtful profitability were constructed and owned by the State.

Britain's dominance of shipping and shipbuilding

With government support, and making good use of contemporary science, the submarine cable industry maintained a position of world leadership. The other vital element of Imperial communications was the steamship. This, too, was part of a British-dominated industry during those closing decades of the nineteenth century when radio was developing.

Table 1.2 compares the tonnages of the main ship-owning nations. The British lead was nearly as marked as it was for submarine cables. Indeed, that lead is underestimated, as the figures for the USA include vessels employed on the Great Lakes and in coastal trade.

Table 1.2 *Merchant shipping (million tonnes gross)*
(% of world total in brackets)

	1873	1890	1900
Britain	7·59 (43·3%)	11·60 (52·3%)	14·26 (49·1%)
USA	2·50 (14·3%)	1·83 (8·3%)	2·75 (9·5%)
Italy	1·14 (6·5%)	0·82 (3·7%)	0·98 (3·4%)
Norway	1·11 (6·3%)	1·58 (7·2%)	1·47 (5·1%)
Germany	1·03 (5·9%)	1·57 (7·1%)	2·65 (9·1%)
France	1·01 (5·8%)	1·05 (4·7%)	1·35 (4·7%)

Source: Watts, *Ship*, p. 875.

This huge merchant fleet was supported by the world's largest ship-building industry. Annual outputs of British shipyards increased from about 343,000 tonnes gross in 1870 to more than 1,509,000 tonnes gross in 1900. This latter figure represents sixty-five per cent of the whole world's construction for the year. It was a much greater percentage than the proportion of merchant ships then under British ownership.[6] The discrepancy was due to a profitable export trade; a significant part even of the German merchant fleet was built in Britain.

Shipbuilding was, unlike the submarine cable telegraph, an industry which had existed for centuries. British yards retained practices developed long before there was any thought of applying scientific techniques to determine whether they were the best methods available. But, as Hobsbawn has shown,[7] they were not noticeably inferior to foreign competitors in this respect. The industry was organised, world-wide, very much on traditional lines. Mass-production and similar advanced management techniques were not introduced until the twentieth century. Shipbuilders had no need to learn new methods nor to raise capital for new machinery in order to remain competitive. But this conservatism did not apply to all sectors of the industry. There were important changes in the design and construction of the ships themselves.

Competition for the world's trade resulted in orders for merchant ships which were becoming larger and more complex. For example, the original *Oceanic*, launched at Belfast in 1871, was an iron passenger vessel of 7,240 tonnes displacement, with engines that developed 3,000 ihp at a steam pressure of $4\cdot6$ kg/cm^2. The replacement ship of the same name, a steelbuilt liner, was launched in 1899; this vessel displaced 26,100 tonnes, with machinery generating 29,000 ihp at a steam pressure of $13\cdot5$ kg/cm^2. Indeed, the last three decades of the nineteenth century were a time of continual innovation. The output of steamships from British yards overtook that of sailing vessels in about 1870. Steel construction replaced wood and iron from 1880 onwards. Triple-expansion compound engines came into general use after about 1885 (steam turbines were not fitted in large ships before the twentieth century). Such changes in size, power and materials could not be achieved simply by modifications of traditional techniques. The industry had to accept – and to initiate – studies in applied science to achieve the improvements which its customers demanded. For instance, British shipbuilders sponsored most research into the electrochemistry of corrosion during the nineteenth century,[8] and the adoption of the Whitworth screw thread, perhaps the most important example of standardisation in the history of mechanical engineering, was largely due to the shipbuilding industry.

The industry never achieved such a close association of science and engineering as existed in the submarine cable companies. But the level of government support was greater, and rather more apparent, than that enjoyed by the cable industry. Some support was provided by contracts to private yards for the construction of warships for the Royal Navy. These contracts were an important source of finance.[9] They also supplied detailed designs and specifications as a means of introducing the latest scientifically-based techniques into the industry. Further government subsidies were provided for merchant ships built to Admiralty specifications, to be taken over by the Royal Navy in event of war. But the most important contribution was the government's own direct involvement in shipbuilding. The State-owned Royal Dockyards built most of the battleships and other large vessels for the Royal Navy. Private yards concentrated (so far as warships were concerned) on orders for cruisers, scouts and torpedo boats.

These dockyards were supported from the mid-1880s by an organisation to ensure that warships were built to high standards. In 1882, the Controller of the Navy (responsible for supply of the Royal Navy's equipment) was brought into the Board of Admiralty. The Controller took the title of Third Naval Lord with the status and authority appropriate to the highest councils of naval policy. Engineering schools at Portsmouth, Plymouth and Greenwich became centres for the Royal Navy's research into applied science. Their standards drew envious comment from at least one engineer officer of the United States' Navy.[10] Nor were the needs of technicians and craftsmen ignored. On the contrary, the apprentice schools of the Royal Dockyards were recognised as the best introduction to a career in shipbuilding. Allocation of public funds to these training schools for the Royal Navy, the Royal Corps of Naval Constructors and the Royal Dockyards was a substantial addition to government investment in the scientific education and research supporting the Empire's communications industries. Scientifically-trained officers from the Royal Navy's schools were to make important contributions to the development of radio telegraphy.

The Royal Navy as defender of the Empire's communications

In addition to aiding the nation's shipbuilders, the Royal Navy was directly responsible for the defence of Imperial communications. This had been the Fleet's implicit duty for more than a hundred years. It was not, however, defined explicitly in strategic discussions until the late nineteenth century. The debate began in 1868 when Sir John Colomb (1838–1909) suggested that land-based defence would be ineffective against a blockade of the nation's trade routes. The government's Milne Committee was appointed in 1878 to study the problems of colonial defence. This committee argued that Colomb's view of modern naval warfare meant frontiers extending to the furthest limits of the Empire.[11] Thereafter, the concept of centralised Imperial government was to include the concept of centralised nautical defence.

Recognising the Royal Navy's responsibility for the defence of Imperial communications did not mean the task could be fulfilled easily. A few fast enemy cruisers could move freely about the vast area of the world's oceans. Easily evading detection, they would be free to intercept cargo steamers whenever no British warships were in sight. No solution was found to this problem during the nineteenth century, despite considerable discussion and exercises by the Royal Navy. The best proposal was to confine merchant ships to a limited number of well-defined routes in time of war. Fast passenger liners could be taken over and converted into auxiliary cruisers to patrol these routes during a conflict.[12] Defence of the submarine cables appeared to be an easier task. It was assumed that the Royal Navy could prevent enemy ships grappling for cables at sea and would be summoned to protect island stations. All that seemed necessary therefore was the elimination of cable stations sited on foreign (and potentially hostile) territory. Accordingly several cables were moved or relaid during the 1890s – from Britain to Mauritius in 1893, to Hong Kong in 1894, to the West Indies in 1898 and to South Africa in 1900 – so that all their stations were in British colonies.

But there were doubts about the Fleet's capacity to carry out these duties. As shown in Table 1.3, by 1888 the numerical superiority which the Royal Navy enjoyed in the years of wooden sailing warships had ended. A naval alliance between France and Russia would leave Britain with clear superiority only in the numbers of battleships. And even this superiority could be eliminated by rapid mobilisation while British ships were detached to distant stations.

Table 1.3 *Warships in commission*

	Battleships	Cruisers	Torpedo boats
Britain	42	59	143
France	22	51	111
Russia	2	23	92

Source: Parliamentary Returns: Fleets, Great Britain and Foreign Countries; 1888.

The Franco-Russian alliance became a reality with the signing of a formal military convention on 4 January 1894. Britain anticipated this move by opening informal discussions for naval co-operation with Italy. Squadrons of the Royal Navy visited Genoa in February 1888 and Venice in July 1891. But this was not enough to satisfy the demands of many naval officers. Foreign allies could not be expected to protect all of Britain's interests. Security of the Empire's trade and communications, they claimed, needed a fleet outclassing any combination of two foreign navies. Fisher,[13] a gunnery expert who had commanded a battleship at the bombardment of Alexandria, was a particularly vociferous exponent of their views. He argued that the Admiralty should ensure Britain's naval supremacy for several years by building large numbers of new warships. His emphasis on advanced technology for such ships was criticised by some other officers. They believed that naval thinking on material topics neglected such matters as personnel morale and strategic planning. Fisher's views, however, were an important element in British naval policy for the next twenty years. He had the invaluable assistance of the influential journalist W. T. Stead[14] in the early years of his campaign. In September 1884, Stead began publishing articles in the *Pall Mall Gazette* advocating the naval reforms which Fisher proposed. From 1888, another reformist journal, the *Fortnightly Review*, added its support to the campaign. The cause was then taken up in the House of Commons by a radical Liberal member, Sir Charles Dilke.[15]

There was a great deal of influential support for the campaign. The prestige of the Royal Navy was very high during the nineteenth century. It had protected the country against foreign invasion during the Napoleonic Wars; it had been the means in practice of suppressing piracy and the slave trade when so decreed by the nation's politicians and humanitarian reformers; it was the principle instrument which had secured and sustained the overseas Empire. All influential social and political groups could find at least one aspect of the country's naval policy which merited their approval. Several political pressure groups were set up to work for the Royal Navy's expansion. The most important was the Navy League, founded in 1895. It numbered several Members of Parliament and other prominent political activists among its membership. There were more of these politicians from the Conservative Party than any other. All the same, the representation of Liberals and other reformists was large enough to justify the League's claim to be non-partisan. The women's movement was well represented, and once proposed financing a battleship to be presented to the Fleet on behalf of 'the women of Britain'. Well-known Socialists like Hyndman and Kier Hardie, although not members of the League, endorsed its policy. The shipbuilding industry, both the owners and the Trades Unions representing its employees, naturally had a vested interest in the League's success.[16]

Political debate and the polemic outpourings of these pressure groups combined to create a public awareness of contemporary nautical matters. Wiener claims that a 'rural myth' inhibited the development of British industry. Imperialism was the antithesis, stimulating those industries like shipbuilding, cables and radio telegraphy which contributed to overseas communications. And for many people, the concept of Imperialism was manifested as a 'maritime myth'. This myth related national status (a conveniently vague idea for the popular orator or music-hall entertainer, as it was unquantifiable) to the size and quality of the Royal Navy and merchant fleet. It was a romanticised, even a naive version of the realities of sea power and commerce. But it was effective. Its influence extended even into the nation's literature and music. Such works as Kipling's *A Fleet in Being* (1898), Hardy's *The Dynasts* (1904/1908), Newbolt's *Songs of the Fleet* (1904) and Wood's *Fantasia of British Sea Songs* (1905), as well as the many books and magazines intended for younger people helped to perpetuate this 'maritime myth'. And its effects were reinforced by the scientifically-trained officers who advised the naval correspondents of the national press. Informing the public about details of marine engineering, they helped promulgate Fisher's technological view of naval efficiency. While industry in general might neglect applied science, the press regularly reported developments which might be utilised in warships or cargo vessels. Advanced technology, like radio telegraphy, interested both public and Parliament if it were of any use at sea. And there was such a use for radio during the late nineteenth century. For both the Royal Navy and the mercantile marine had discovered an urgent need for a new wireless communication system.

References

1   G. R. M. Garratt, *One Hundred Years of Submarine Cables*, London, The Science Museum, 1950, pp. 38–9; E. Garcke, 'Telegraphy', *Encyclopaedia Britannica*, 11th edition, 1911, pp. 528–9; S. G. Sturmey, *The Economic Development of Radio*, London, Duckworth, 1958, pp. 75–6.

2   Strictly, he was still known as William Thomson during most of his partnership with Bright, as he was not raised to the peerage until 1892. I have, however, used his title throughout to avoid any confusion with Elihu Thomson and Silvanus Thompson, both of whom are also mentioned in this narrative.

3   Quoted by R. Appleyard, *The History of the Institution of Electrical Engineers, 1871–1931*, London, I.E.E., 1939, p. 55.

4   J. W. and J. Brett to Sir Robert Peel, 23 July 1845, quoted by Garratt, *Submarine Cables*, p. 8.

5   Garcke, *Telegraphy*, p. 529.

6   P. Watts, 'Ship,' *Encyclopaedia Britannica*, 11th edition, 1911, p. 873.

7   E. J. Hobsbawm, *Industry and Empire*, Harmondsworth, Penguin, 1969, pp. 178–9.

8   C. A. Smith, 'The corrosion story', *Anti-Corrosion*, XXIV, 1977, pp. 12–15.

9   A. J. Marder, *The Anatomy of British Sea Power: A History of British Naval Policy in the Pre-Dreadnought Era, 1880–1905*, London, Frank Cass & Co., 1964, p. 25, cites *The Iron and Coal Trades Review*, for 13 March 1896 to the effect that work on warships cost £27 per ton weight, as against £6 per ton weight average for all iron and steel products.

10   F. C. Bieg, 'On the necessity and value of scientific research in naval engineering matters,' *Journal of the American Society of Naval Engineers*, 1895, reprinted in *The Naval Engineers' Journal*, XCVI, 1984, pp. 87–9.

11   K. D. Logan, *The Admiralty: Reforms and Reorganisation, 1868–1892*, PhD Thesis, University of Oxford, 1976, p. 286.

12   Marder, *British Sea Power*, p. 96.

13   Later Admiral of the Fleet Lord Fisher of Kilverstone (1841–1920), First Sea Lord 1903–1909 and 1914–15, Chairman of the Admiralty's Inventions Board, 1916–18.

14   W. T. Stead (1849–1912) was one of the best-known journalists on the radical wing of Liberal politics, famous for his press campaigns against the Bulgarian atrocities in 1877 and against child prostitution in 1885. His reputation as an anti-Imperialist was due to his attitudes during the Boer War in 1899–1902 and had no influence on his campaigns for a strengthened fleet in 1884. An active spiritualist (as were several contemporary radio engineers) Stead was drowned in the wreck of the *Titanic* on 15 April 1912 – a disaster which itself prompted a great increase in the use of radio in merchant ships.

15   Marder, *British Sea Power*, pp. 120–40.

16   *Ibid*, pp. 35, 49–55.

2

A naval problem

... the urgent necessity of some system of recognition signals between ships and boats.   Captain B. W. Walker, RN, 1984

The organisation of the Royal Navy in the late nineteenth century resembled that of the Empire which it served. Its warships were stationed in all parts of the world; centralised control was exercised ultimately from the Admiralty in London. Civil servants and uniformed officers at the Admiralty communicated with bases in Britain by inland telegraph and with local commanders at overseas stations through the submarine cables. Electric telegraphs were used generally for the transmission of naval instructions and information by 1880. The bombardment of Alexandria in July 1882 — the first action fought by steam-powered ironclad ships of the Royal Navy — was initiated and monitored closely from London by telegraphic communication.[1]

But while the Admiralty could use the latest communications technology, commanders at sea were less well equipped. Communications between individual ships still depended on developments of the flag signals that had been in use in Nelson's time. In February 1867, Colomb[2] introduced a system of flashing light signals similar to the familiar Morse code. An admiral in his flagship could then keep in touch with his fleet, by day and by night. But this was possible only while the weather were good and all ships were within visual range.

Communications within and between ships

The problems of communication in poor weather were emphasised in 1875 by the collision in fog between HMS *Vanguard* and HMS *Iron Duke*. At the subsequent court of enquiry, the captain of HMS *Iron Duke* was exonerated for holding his course. The captain of HMS *Vanguard*, conversely, was censured for altering course without orders (although he had attempted to advise other vessels of his intentions with sound signals on the ship's siren). Communication between commander and subordinates was a matter of instant unquestioning obedience to simple unambiguous orders. Ultimate responsibilities of the local commander were defined clearly under such a structure. The centralisation of authority within the Royal Navy was an exaggerated instance of a general tendency to centralised authority already evident in Britain.

This tendency to resort to stricter hierarchical discipline as a solution to communications problems was exacerbated by technological changes. Armour plate was introduced for warships in mid-century; each increase in thickness of armour induced designers to install larger guns as a counter in the following generation of vessels. But mounting larger guns meant that fewer could be carried in each ship.[3] Effective use of the armament then depended on greater accuracy and consequently a more precise control of the guns' crews. The gunnery school, HMS *Excellent*, became famous − or more correctly notorious among naval ratings − as a centre of drill and discipline. Heavier guns increased the effective ranges at which, it was anticipated, naval battles would be fought in the future. And advances in steam machinery were making appreciable improvements in warships' speeds and endurance. These changes increased the effective radius of action of a battlefleet − provided of course, that the individual units in the fleet did not stray beyond the range of their Admiral's signals.

The annual manoeuvres for 1888 revealed the limitations of existing communications methods. Official strategy was still based on the concept of a close blockade of an enemy's fleet in its ports. This strategy was tested by the manoeuvres, which lasted from 24 July to 20 August 1888. The 'foreign' forces, of an imaginary enemy called 'Achille', were divided into two squadrons: five battleships and five cruisers were at Berehaven, another four battleships and five cruisers were at Lough Swilly. This fleet was to attempt to escape from its ports, combine its two squadrons and carry out a mock invasion of the mainland. The 'friendly' A Fleet were instructed to frustrate this plan by maintaining an effective blockade.[4]

The results were disturbing. Six cruisers and a battleship from the 'Achille' force managed to evade the blockade and assemble at a prearranged rendezvous. Carrying out a series of simulated raids on coastal towns, they obliged the Admiral commanding A Fleet to withdraw his forces and protect the Channel. Subsequent analysis suggested the 'Achille' success was due, at least in part, to the use of the electric telegraph for co-ordinating tactics at their two bases. Blockading ships at sea could not communicate so rapidly while the separate squadrons were out of sight of each other.[5]

Squadrons at sea then relied for long-distance communication on the use of fast torpedo boats as dispatch vessels. *Torpedo Boat No 81*, commanded by Lieutenant Henry Jackson,[6] was used in this role by A Fleet. Jackson was detached from the main force on 7 August to circulate instructions for the concentration of the Fleet's individual squadrons. He was ordered to sail to Falmouth and there to contact the squadrons' various bases by telegraph. However, his torpedo boat was delayed by fog. He was several hours late in reaching Falmouth and the 'Achille' ships gained a corresponding advantage.[7] Even the fastest dispatch vessels could not pass orders to other ships at sea or to shore with the rapidity and reliability of the electric telegraph. Torpedo-boats possessed a useful margin of speed over other vessels. But they were not able to solve the problems of ship-to-shore or ship-to-ship communication. Indeed, they had themselves created new communications problems for the Royal Navy.

Trials with torpedo-boats

Smaller and faster than other warships, torpedo-boats were a new element in naval strategy during the later nineteenth century. They could be built more quickly and for far less cost than the smallest cruisers. A difficult target for enemy gunners, they carried weapons which might disable the most powerful battleship. France and Russia were known to be building these boats in large numbers. Their torpedo flotillas might well represent the greatest threat to the British battle-fleet in any future conflict.

In 1872 the old wooden frigate HMS *Vernon* was attached to the gunnery school as torpedo training ship. Four years later, the HMS *Vernon* establishment was set up as an independent torpedo school. It studied technology and tactics associated with torpedo operations both in offence and defence. Torpedo defences at that time were based mainly on the use of searchlights (energised by dynamos from the ships' steam systems) and submarine mines (energised by primary cells), which were the first applications of electric power in warships.

Consequently, the school soon became the Royal Navy's centre for electrical research and development.

By the late 1880s, Jackson and his colleagues on the school's staff had discovered particular problems in communicating with and between torpedo boats. Special trials in the Mediterranean had revealed difficulties when signalling between torpedo boats and other ships in darkness. The most significant trial, on the night of 13 April 1887, was a simulated attack against a battle squadron at anchor. Six battleships – HMS *Alexandra*, HMS *Colossus*, HMS *Dreadnought*, HMS *Polyphemus*, HMS *Temeraire* and HMS *Thunderer* – were stationed in Livathi Bay, Cephalonia, for this exercise. They were protected by several lines of defence to reveal any attacking vessel before it approached to within torpedo range. There were two lines of guard boats (steam pinnaces and rowing boats) covering the entrance to the bay and two sets of fixed searchlights to provide additional lighting when an enemy ship was identified.[8]

The torpedo boats – eight in all – attacked in two divisions with an interval of three minutes between them. Contemporary reports suggest that there was considerable confusion during this action, despite the carefully prepared defences. Although the attacking torpedo boats showed up clearly in the searchlights' beams, they were obscured by gunsmoke as soon as the defending ships opened fire with blank rounds. The situation was further complicated by the lack of an agreed code of signals for the guard boats. Captain E. F. Jeffreys, reporting on the lessons learned from the exercise, commented:

when the attack commenced, each boat appeared to be throwing up as many signals as possible ... For the purpose of signalling an enemy blue or long lights are objectionable as they show up the boat signalling, whilst the difficulty of firing rockets can only be appreciated by those who have had to signal from boats in rough or wet weather.[9]

In other words, it was not possible to signal to a friendly vessel without thereby revealing the ship's position to an enemy. For the same reason, commanders of small boats in the outlying defences were unwilling to challenge approaching vessels at night. Commander E. P. Gallwey, who commanded the attacking torpedo boats during the exercise, confirmed these findings in his own report:

I am inclined to think that when the guard-boats are not so distant from their ship as to prevent coloured or flashing lights being seen that these latter may often be used with advantage, as the guard boats are then able to give warning to the fleet without revealing their own positions.[10]

The operation of torpedo-boats, in attack or (as guard boats and dispatch vessels) in defence of larger ships, had created a need for a new means of communication. Ships' commanders required signals which did not betray a ship's position, especially at night or in the smoke created by heavy guns. The exercises had shown, however, that the confusion of a torpedo assault disrupted the defence more than the attacking force. Any French or Russian admirals who learned of these results (or discovered them in exercises of their own devising) would have regarded them as confirmation of their strategic plans. But the Royal Navy anticipated that future naval wars might involve many attacks by flotillas of foreign torpedo craft against their battlefleet. There was an urgent need to find some method of communication which would restore their advantage.

Recognition of the communications problems

The officers at the torpedo school analysed the results of the 1887 exercises carefully before initiating any specific research project. Captain S. Long, the Commanding Officer, recommended that ships should be fitted with 'improved searchlights as they are important for defence of a mine field when fog or smoke prevent artillery fire playing on it, and for the defence of a fleet against torpedo boats' and also that 'The work of guarding a fleet should be systematically practised, and every effort should be made to obtain some satisfactory plan of identifying friends and distinguishing them from foes.'[11] The school had not, therefore, identified a need for an entirely new method of signalling as early as 1887. Long's report suggests that they were still thinking of codes and modifications of existing devices to solve the communications problem.

But the experiences of torpedo craft during the 1888 manoeuvres emphasised that there was a new problem. A cruiser squadron engaged, and was deemed to have destroyed, two of their own torpedo boats.[12] Existing lamps and flares were obviously inadequate. Speeds of warships and the destructive ranges of weapons had increased so that faster methods of distinguishing friendly from enemy ships were essential. As the introductory remarks to the torpedo school's annual report for 1888 admitted:

No perfectly satisfactory method of distinguishing between friendly and hostile torpedo boats appears yet to have been devised, and no ship could in war allow a torpedo boat to approach her on a dark night. It would appear very difficult for a torpedo boat to identify an enemy without exposing herself to destruction.[13]

There was no practical progress towards a solution of the problem for several years.

This lack of progress was emphasised by further exercises with torpedo boats in the Mediterranean during December 1892. Familiar difficulties of co-ordinating movements of ships at night without displaying lights to betray their positions to enemy vessels were again reported by officers supervising the trials. Vice-Admiral Sir George Tryon (1832–93), the fleet's Commander-in-Chief, singled out the communication problem for mention in his own report:

The value of establishing communications by telephone or Morse sounders with electric light stations, batteries and look-out stations is established, and when necessary to make general signals to a squadron it will be preferable to make them from a central station on shore than from ship to ship, thus revealing their positions ...[14]

Although emphasising the utility of the most modern technological devices, Tryon was therefore making no new suggestions about the problem. His main contribution was simply to acknowledge the need for better communications. He was the most senior officer – and a very respected officer – to identify a need for a further research. In the Royal Navy's hierarchical structure, the support of a Vice-Admiral was an invaluable asset.

But, sadly, Tryon was not to exert his influence for very long. On 22 June 1893, he was leading the Mediterranean Fleet off the Syrian coast. The battleships were deployed in two parallel columns when Tryon gave the order to reverse course, each ship turning inwards in succession. It was evident to many officers present that the columns were too close for such a manoeuvre to be performed safely. But no one dared override an Admiral's order. By the time that Tryon himself realised his error it was too late to pass a countermanding instruction. The leading vessels of the columns, HMS *Camperdown* and Tryon's flagship, HMS *Victoria*, continued to turn towards each other and collided. HMS *Victoria* sank in a few minutes; 359 seamen, including Tryon himself, died in the wreck. It was a tragic illustration of the failings that were possible in ship-to-ship communications. Even when working with experienced well-disciplined sailors under conditions of good visibility fatal mistakes could occur. It seemed that nothing less than a signalling system involving an entirely new technology would solve the Royal Navy's problems.

Logan's study of Admiralty policy in the later nineteenth century mentions the hostility of some older officers to the emphasis on technology among the younger generation.[15] But this younger generation ultimately carried the day. Fisher, who initiated the campaign for a stronger Fleet, was brought onto the Board of Admiralty as Controller in 1892. Dilke, the politician most closely associated with the campaign, forced the unwilling Gladstone to concede a large increase in the Navy Estimates for 1893.[16]

The officers at the torpedo school, HMS *Vernon*, (which had originally been commanded by Fisher himself) were mostly of this younger generation. They were enthusiastic advocates of using technology to solve tactical problems. Their commanding officer, Captain B.W. Walker (who had succeeded Long), reminded them of 'the urgent necessity of some system of recognition signals between ships and boats. The problem, which is one of great difficulty, has been referred to the *Vernon* for solution.'[17]

As the torpedo school was the Royal Navy's centre of electrical expertise, it was evident that their eventual solution would utilise electrical apparatus. The general trend of these torpedo officers' thoughts on the problem was apparent by the summer of 1895. Electric telegraph instruments were then used successfully for communication between ships of the Mediterranean Fleet while at anchor.[18] It was, however, obvious that the inter-connecting cables made such telegraphic apparatus unsuitable for communication between ships under way. What was needed was, in a general sense, a wire*less* telegraph without any material conductor between transmitter and receiver.

The work of the electrical engineers in the torpedo school was mostly unknown to their civilian contemporaries. Reports from the torpedo school were usually classified as 'Confidential', which limited their distribution to those involved in the studies. In fact no details of the torpedo-boat trials have been published before this present study. But naval officers could keep abreast of developments ouside the Service, if these developments were mentioned in the technical press. They would have known that, by 1895, they were investigating part of a general maritime signalling problem that also concerned civilian telegraph engineers. While the Royal Navy was losing capital ships like HMS *Victoria* on the high seas, problems of civil maritime communication were demonstrated in equally dramatic fashion. The coastal rescue services found existing methods of communication to be inadequate in bad weather. Civilian engineers, adapting modern technology for safety at sea, had also discovered the need for a reliable wireless telegraph.[19] And their findings could be reported and discussed by the public press.

References

1 A. Hezlet, *'The Electron and the Sea Power,'* London, Peter Davies, 1975, pp. 18–19.
2 Captain (later Admiral Sir Philip) Colomb, RN (1811–99), brother to Sir John Colomb, was one of the founders of the Society of Telegraph Engineers in 1871.
3 The Royal Navy's first steam-powered, armoured warship, HMS *Warrior* (launched in 1860), carried twenty-eight guns of 18 cm calibre and had armour 11 cm thick. HMS *Benbow* (of 1885) had virtually the same overall linear dimensions, but carried only two guns, of 40 cm calibre, and armour 43 cm thick.
4 'Extracts from the Report of the Committee on the Naval Manoeuvres', 1888, pp. 38–40 (NHL).
5 A. J. Marder, *The Anatomy of British Sea Power: a History of British Naval Policy in the Pre-Dreadnought Era, 1880–1905*, London, Frank Cass & Co., 1964, pp. 105–16.
6 Later Admiral of the Fleet Sir Henry Bradwardine Jackson (1855–1929), First Sea Lord 1915–16 and the first Chairman of the Radio Research Board, 1920–27.
7 'Committee on Naval Manoeuvres', p. 46.
8 'Annual Report of the Torpedo School (HMS *Vernon*)' for 1887, pp. 135–50 (NHL).
9 *Ibid*, p. 143.
10 *Ibid*, p. 146.
11 *Ibid*, p. 149.
12 'Committee on Naval Manoeuvres', p. 13.
13 'Annual Report of the Torpedo School (HMS *Vernon*), for 1888, p. 8 (NHL).
14 'Annual Report of the Torpedo School (HMS *Vernon*), for 1893, p. 174 (NHL).
15 K. D. Logan, *The Admiralty: Reforms and Reorganisation, 1868–1892*, PhD Thesis, University of Oxford, 1976, p. 268.
16 Marder, *British Sea Power*, pp. 135–40.
17 'Annual Report of the Torpedo School (HMS *Vernon*)', for 1894, pp. ix–x (NHL).

18 'Annual Report of the Torpedo School (HMS *Vernon*)', for 1895, p. 115 (NHL).

19 It is not an anachronism to use the term 'wireless telegraph' in this context; the expression was commonly employed, even before the invention of radio, to describe telegraphs without connecting wires between transmitter and receiver.

3

Public concern

... the duty of the State to watch over the safety of her sailors.

The Times, 1892

During the latter half of the nineteenth century, the coastal rescue services introduced new technical devices comparable with those in merchant vessels and warships. These innovations can conveniently be considered to date from about 1850. The National Lifeboat Institution (founded in 1824) was then re-organised and accepted responsibility for the work of local lifeboat stations and committees. The first self-righting lifeboat was designed in 1851, in response to an Institution competition; the first steam-powered lifeboat was introduced in 1890. Various other items of safety equipment were being modified over the same period, notably the line-carrying rocket, used from 1855 onwards, and the improved life belt introduced in 1898.

While the rescue services were being modernised, the parallel services for maintaining lighthouses and lightships underwent a similar transformation. In 1854, the Mercantile Marine Act placed Trinity House (and a few smaller lighthouse authorities) under the supervision of the Board of Trade. Their technical effort in the late nineteenth century concentrated on improving the lighting and fog signals. A recent history suggests that concern for economy may have persuaded lighthouse authorities to seek solutions to technical problems based on traditional practices rather than research.[1] The scientific input to the work of Trinity House was, however, increased after 1866. The physicist John Tyndall (1820–93) was then appointed scientific adviser to the Board of Trade. He was very active with experiments to determine the best foghorns and lighthouse illuminants, but resigned in 1883 after a prolonged dispute with James Douglass, the Board's chief engineer.

But the coastal safety and rescue services had the same problem as the Royal Navy. Their communications systems had not been developed to the same technological standards as much of their other equipment. This deficiency in offshore communications became public knowledge when the mail steamer *Schiller* was wrecked on the Retarrier Reef, west of the Scilly Isles, on the night of Friday 7 May 1875. It was admitted by survivors that 'a rejoicing on a small scale had been indulged in honour of the birthday of one of the officers'. Nevertheless, they claimed, 'the working of the ship was in no way neglected'.[2] Instead, they blamed the navigational error which caused the accident on thick fog. There had been a panic which involved some of the crew. Three hundred and twelve lives were lost.

Shipwreck was then by no means unusual. In fact, it was sufficiently common during the 1870s to justify a daily column of 'Shipping Disasters' in *The Times*. But the high death toll from the *Schiller* — and the high proportion of the crew rescued, while many passengers died — attracted especial attention in the national press. Some commentators discussed possible modifications to existing procedures to improve safety while navigating off a dangerous coast. Others, including Kelvin, emphasised the need for better communications at night and in fog. Two residents of the Scillies made particularly pertinent comments from their local knowledge. F. Banfield revealed that there was no telegraph for the lifeboat station at St Mary's; J. C. Uren agreed and added direct evidence that a telegraph might well have been the means of saving many lives.[3] The keepers of the Bishop Rock lighthouse had, according to Uren, been witnesses of the accident. Towards morning, as the light improved, they had seen many survivors still alive, clinging to flotsam from the wreck. But there was no telegraph linking the lighthouse with the shore. The unhappy keepers had no means of alerting either local fishermen or the lifeboat station some ten kilometres distant. They were obliged to remain passive spectators of the tragedy.

Coastal communications, in the widest sense of the term, were all then controlled by government agencies. The observation of vessels off shore was the duty of the coastguard and consequently of the Admiralty. Transmission of warning signals from lighthouses and foghorns was the responsibility of Trinity House and ultimately of the Board of Trade. Similarly, the provision and maintenance of coastal telegraph lines (and offshore within territorial waters) devolved on the General Post Office. These examples of centralisation of authority had not existed for very long at the time of the *Schiller* disaster. The lighthouse service had been brought under the Board of

Trade in 1855, while the telegraphs were nationalised in 1870. Nevertheless, this state-control was tacitly accepted by most of those interested in offshore safety. Even the National Lifeboat Institution, which then, as now, was supported entirely by voluntary contributions and prided itself on its independence, did not question it. The Institution's members accepted that coastal communications were properly the government's responsibility. Most of them probably concurred with the anonymous author of an editorial article on the subject in the Institution's journal:

... such a labour could of course only be undertaken by the State, and no private society, or commercial body, or national institution could by any means interfere with a work which, both on account of the utilisation of the means already existing, and of the indispensable control it would be necessary to hold over numerous individuals on all parts of the coast, must of necessity be initiated, carried out, and kept under due supervision by the Government.[4]

This acceptance of government-controlled communications may have been influenced by publicity for the Merchant Shipping Bill. The state of many unseaworthy 'coffin ships' in Britain's merchant marine had been exposed in Plimsoll's book *Our Seamen: an Appeal* (1873). But the Bill to remedy the problem was not introduced into Parliament until July 1875. This was just over a month after the wreck of the *Schiller*, while the accident was still a subject for discussion. The passage of this Bill provided seamen with protection similar to the various Factory Acts and Public Health Acts which regulated conditions for factory workers. Several public meetings approved resolutions supporting this extension of centralised State control to include provision for safety at sea.

But recognition of State responsibility, through the Post Office, for coastal telegraphs did not mean this responsibility was being discharged effectively. While the *Life-Boat Journal* favoured State control of coastal communications, it was extremely critical of the State's existing work. The coastal communications network had, it claimed, deteriorated even as the performance of signalling systems improved. A semaphore service was set up as part of the coastal defences during the Napoleonic Wars. This had still been available for the coastguard service at the end of hostilities. Eventually, the semaphore system had fallen into disuse with the introduction of the electric telegraph. But the concentration of lines in areas of large population (and, consequently, profitable traffic) meant that the telegraph network radiated from inland cities. There were few telegraph links along the coastline. As the journal put it, there was 'greater difficulty in communicating along the coast and summoning aid to distressed vessels at all out-of-the-way parts of the coast, than existed at the end of the [eighteenth] century'.[5]

Two aspects of coastal telegraphy needed improvements – connections between the mainland system and offshore structures such as lighthouses and lightships, as indentified by Uren in his letter to *The Times*, and telegraphic links to the more remote parts of the coast, as pointed out by Banfield. The former was the greater problem. For one thing, Trinity House objected to telegraphic or any other equipment in lighthouses which might, they claimed, distract keepers from their primary duties.[6] This does not seem, in retrospect, a major difficulty. But, even so, there was no satisfactory equipment existing in the 1880s which could be used in lighthouses and lightships. As Douglass explained, lighthouses were by their nature built on or near rocky reefs. They were subject to violent storms which might be expected to destroy any ordinary cable connection. Lightships were not static terminals, but imposed strains on cable ends with their continual movements. Indeed, an experimental cable installation at the Sunk lightship off the Essex coast failed twice in 1885. One failure was due to flexion from the regular rise and fall of the ship with the tide and waves; the other occurred when the vessel broke loose from its moorings in a gale.

Ideally, an apparatus was needed as reliable and convenient as the electric telegraph but without vulnerable conductors between transmitter and receiver. Such devices had been made experimentally. Several well-known American engineers, including Samuel Morse (1791–1872), Mahlon Loomis (1826–86), and Thomas Edison (1847–1931) had shown it was possible to signal across appreciable distances without connecting wires. Their devices, using mutual induction between two circuits or else the conduction through water or damp earth, were already known generically as 'wireless telegraphs'. Amos Dolbear (1837–1910), a physics teacher, demonstrated his wireless *telephone* to the Society of Telegraph Engineers in London during 1882.[7] Membrs of the Society were invited to listen at the receiver to a verbal and musical performance from Dolbear's assistant in an adjacent room. Despite the apparent success of this demonstration, there is no record of any attempt to exploit the invention commercially.

Such experiments were not confined to the USA. William Preece,[8] assistant Engineer-in-Chief to the General Post Office, operated a wireless telegraph of his own design in regular service during March 1882. The cable across the Solent had broken. Preece substituted copper plates, submerged in the sea, connected into the broken ends. Currents conducted through seawater kept the system working. This arrangement maintained the link between the Isle of Wight and the mainland until the cable was repaired.

But Preece's ideas about wireless telegraphy were soon to be modified. In the same year, Preece learned of the effects of inductive 'cross-talk' on telephone lines. He would later use these effects as the basis of yet another system of wireless telegraphy. A popular book of the period about contemporary electrical engineering gives a useful summary of Preece's observations:

... the United Telephone Company had informed the Post Office that on one occasion a clerk had been able to read a telegraphic message which was being sent from London to Bradford. Underneath the Gray's Inn Road and other streets in London for a distance of two and a quarter miles the Post Office has buried the Bradford wire in an iron pipe two and a half feet below the level of the street. Over the roofs of the houses the United Telephone Company had a wire, which ran parallel to the buried wire for some distance. It could, therefore, only have been by induction that any possible disturbance could have been caused. The distance between the wires was a least eighty feet ... Mr. Preece then tried with some lines near Newcastle-on-Tyne, and was able to distinguish sounds in a telegraph circuit ... After this he succeeded in obtaining disturbances ... over distances as far as four and a half miles ... he found as the result of all his trials that at distances up to about half a mile disturbances due to the passage of telegraphic currents were distinctly noticeable; but that at greater distances the effects were rapidly diminished.[9]

It was, therefore, possible that Post Office engineers might use this or some similar effect in a wireless telegraph for lighthouses and lightships. In any case, they might devise a flexible cable termination that was less vulnerable in offshore installations. Both techniques would, however, require the allocation of sufficient funds for their investigation.

There was no technical difficulty in solving the other coastal communication problem. Apparatus for telegraphic connections to lifeboat stations and other rescue centres in remote districts already existed. Again, funds were needed for the Post Office to install lines and instruments. With the emphasis on centralisation of public services, such funds could be obtained only through pressure on the central government. By the late 1880s, diffuse criticism about the provision of communications for offshore rescue coalesced into a political campaign.

Political pressures for improvement

After a further re-organisation in 1883 (including the acquisition of a prefix to its title), the Royal National Lifeboat Institution was more politically active. Successful lobbying secured an amendment to the Removal of Wrecks Act in 1889, reducing hazards to boats engaged in lifesaving duties. Encouraged by this experience, the Institution renewed its efforts to secure an improvement in coastal communications.

The new campaign started in Plymouth. Early in 1890, the local branch of the RNLI wrote to all other branches about the communications problem. At about the same time, a joint meeting of the Chambers of Commerce of the United Kingdom passed a resolution calling on the government to start construction of a new coastal telegraph network. Admiral Hickey, chairman of the Plymouth branch, presented a petition from 184 branches at the RNLI London offices in February 1890. The national committee responded promptly, establishing a sub-committee to investigate and report what advantages might be expected from better telegraphic connections at lifeboat stations.[10] With three admirals and three Members of Parliament among its eight members, this sub-committee already possessed useful information and contacts in the relevant areas of public life.

A well-organised campaign produced thirteen letters and two leading articles published in *The Times* between October and December 1891. This spate of publications culminated in January 1892 with the production of a polemical pamphlet by Robert Bayly, a member of the Plymouth Chamber of Commerce and of the RNLI local committee. His pamphlet revealed how little improvement there had been in the coastal telegraph network during the twenty years since nationalisation. A series of plans illustrated this theme. On most parts of the coast there were lifeboat, coastguard, and rocket stations, but few telephone or telegraph lines linking these stations into the national network. In Denmark, by contrast, the plans showed that coastal rescue stations had telegraph connections into the national network and also with each other directly.[11] Soon after the publication of Bayly's pamphlet, a further leading article in *The Times* reinforced its message.

This article started by re-stating the essence of the problem and the degree of public support already secured:

It has been abundantly shown ... that no system of telegraphic or telephonic communication worthy of the name exists between the coastguard stations, the lighthouses, and the lightships round our shores ... That the establishment and maintenance of an efficient system of shore cables will cost money, and possibly a good deal of money, is, of course, undeniable. But ... we do not think that the nation, which was so profoundly moved by the Plimsoll agitation, will stop to scrutinise the cost of protecting the lives of its sailors ... Lighthouses are usually built on rocks rising abruptly from the sea, and cables in such sites would be subjected to strains far more severe than those which the shore-ends landed on the rockiest coasts now undergo. Lightships, on the other hand ... twist and wrench cables ... until they snap.[12]

But the writer had no doubt that the problems were soluble, nor where the responsibility lay for their solution:

The difficulties ... undoubtedly exist, but it is hard to believe that, in an age when science has accomplished so much, these would long continue to baffle the skill of our engineers if only the necessary funds were placed at their disposal ... It is the duty of the State to protect the lives of all its citizens, and it is in a special sense the duty of the greatest of maritime powers to watch over the safety of her sailors. The State may therefore fairly undertake some portion of the charge. But the shipowners, the merchants and the underwriters acknowledge that they expect to derive substantial benefit from the system they demand. It seems only reasonable that they should be invited to contribute to the insurance fund.

In other words, the problems of the coastal telegraphs might be solved by the same two means which had contributed so greatly to the success of other systems of overseas communications — applied science and State support.

Early in 1892, Sir Edward Birkbeck, chairman of the RNLI, introduced a resolution in the House of Commons stating that it was 'desirable, with the view of decreasing the loss of life from shipwrecks on the coast, that the Government should provide telephonic and telegraphic communication between all the coastguard stations and signal stations on the coast of the United Kingdom, and on such parts of the coast where there are no coastguard stations that the post offices nearest to the Life-boat stations should be connected'. This resolution was accepted unanimously by the House in April 1892. It was decided in addition to appoint a Royal Commission to consider the means and advantages of connecting lighthouses and lightships into the national telegraph system, and to decide which should be so connected.

Post Office experiments with wireless telegraphy

The Royal Commission on Communication with Lighthouses and Lightships was appointed in June 1892. Birkbeck was the Royal National Lifeboat Institution's delegate. The Post Office was represented by its secretary, J.C. Lamb, and its engineer-in-chief, Edward Graves. Other members came from Trinity House and the Board of Trade. In November 1892, after Graves's death, Preece was appointed engineer-in-chief to the Post Office and accordingly took his place on the Commission.

About a month after Preece's appointment, the Commissioners issued their first report. They selected twenty lighthouses and five lightships as the first to be connected into the mainland telegraph system. These installations were chosen not only for their importance to coastal navigation, but also because there was little difficulty making connections with conventional cables. Three more lighthouses – Caldy, the Tuskar Rock and Lundy Island – were suggested for experiments with what was described as 'communication by a non-continuous cable'.[13] This was presumably a wireless system much the same as that which Preece had used across the Solent in 1882. Such a conductive system was subsequently tested, but at the Needles lighthouse instead of any of those recommended by the Commission.[14]

But the most extensive Post Office trials were not with this conductive device but with an inductive wireless telegraph. It was based on the electro-magnetic induction effects which Preece had observed in telephone wires. The transmitting circuit included a motor-driven circuit breaker that produced a pulsating current at a frequency of about 300 Hz in the main circuit line. This induced a current at the same frequency in the receiver circuit, generating a musical note in a telephone receiver; a Morse key at the transmitter broke this note into the dots and dashes of the Morse code.[15]

Preece proposed to use this apparatus for communicating with lightships, either 'by running a wire along the shore on light poles for a distance of about a mile [1·6 kilometres], and a second wire from stem to stern of the ship, the two acting upon each other inductively through the intervening space', or else by 'running out a light cable from the shore to the ship, terminating in a coil at the bottom of the sea, near the ship, but not attached to it, while another coil is placed on board. These two coils are expected to act inductively, and to give ample sound on telephones by means of rapid alternations.[16]

The system was tested, using the first of these methods, late in 1892 at Lavernock Point, near Cardiff. Signals were exchanged with Flat Holme, in the Bristol Channel, across a range of nearly five kilometres. After this successful beginning, further trials were organised at Conway in 1893, at Loch Ness in 1894 (when wireless *telephone*, as well as telegraph messages were sent over 2½ km of water), and at Arran and Kintyre, again in 1894. A year later the system was used in regular service between the Isle of Mull and the mainland while the cable was broken.

Three years of experience had given encouraging results, but revealed one overwhelming defect. The equipment needed parallel wires at transmitter and receiver comparable in length with the distance to be spanned by its signals. A vessel several kilometres off shore would need receiving and transmitting wires several kilometres long! Obviously, a much more compact apparatus would be required if it were ever to be of use in real lightships.

Preece accordingly tried the second of his proposed methods, replacing the parallel wires with two coils, one being in the lightship and the other on the seabed beneath it. This method was tried in August 1896, in Preece's words, as 'a costly attempt to communicate between Ramsgate and the North Goodwin lightship'.[17] But the costly attempt was a disappointing failure. A few hundred metres of seawater between the coils proved too effective an electro-magnetic screen.[18]

In 1892, Vice-Admiral Tyron had formally recognised the Royal Navy's communications problems; in the same year, Parliament accepted the coastal rescue services' need for improvements in offshore signalling. By 1895, the Royal Navy's officers had decided that conventional techniques were unsuitable for ship-to-ship signalling. A year later, Preece found that existing telegraphs could not be modified for use with offshore light vessels. Both the Royal Navy and the Post Office were seeking a new communications technology.

References

1   R.M. MacLeod, 'Science and government in Victorian England: lighthouse illumination and the Board of Trade, 1866–1886', *Isis*, LX, 1969, pp. 5–38.

2   *The Times*, 10 May 1875.

3   *Ibid*, 15 May 1875.

4 Anon, 'Communication by electric telegraph and signals on the coast', *The Life-Boat Journal*, IX, 1876, p. 441.

5 *Ibid*, p. 438.

6 Anon, 'Lighthouses, telegraphs and fog signals', *The Life-Boat Journal*, IX, 1875, p. 367.

7 A. E. Dolbear, 'On the development of a new telephonic system', *Journal of the Society of Telegraph Engineers*, XI, 1882, pp. 130–49.

8 Sir William Henry Preece FRS (1934–1913), Engineer-in-Chief and Electrician to the GPO 1892–99. President of the Institution of Electrical Engineers in 1880 and 1893. President of the Institution of Civil Engineers in 1898.

9 H. Frith and W. S. Rawson, *Coil and Current, or the Triumphs of Electricity*, London, Ward Lock [1896], pp. 239–42.

10 *The Life-Boat Journal*, XIV, 1890, pp. 410–11.

11 R. Bayly, *Electrical Communication on the Coasts of the United Kingdom*, Plymouth Chamber of Commerce, 1892 (NMM, ref. P. 262).

12 *The Times*, 12 January 1892.

13 *The Life-Boat Journal*, XV, 1893, p. 514.

14 W. S. Smith, 'Transmission of electrical signals through space', *The Electrician*, XXXI, 1893, pp. 589–90.

15 J. Gavey, 'Report by Engineer-in Chief of Post Office on Technical Aspect of Wireless Telegraphy', 1903, (PO, File Eng 26411/03, p. 2).

16 *The Times*, 22 November 1892.

17 *Daily Telegraph*, 14 December 1896.

18 Gavey, 'Report on Wireless Telegraphy', p. 4.

4

The Post Office response

... I cannot recall ... one single instance where I have derived any benefit from pure theory ...   W.H. Preece, 1888

The inductive telegraph had not solved the maritime communications problem. But it can now be recognised, with hindsight, that a more practical method of wireless telegraphy had already been proposed. This suggestion of what would later be called a radio telegraph was made by Alexander Pelham Trotter (1857–1947). In 1891, when the campaign for improved coastal communications was under way, Trotter wrote in *The Electrician* about Hertz's discovery of electromagnetic waves with properties similar to visible light. Moreover, Trotter suggested how these invisible electromagnetic waves might eventually be used in an offshore telegraph:

The obvious way of communication between a lightship or a lighthouse would be by flash signals, but a slight mist would effectually stop the beam of light. Hertz has shown how slower vibrations may be received and observed ... These radiations would probably pierce not only fog but a brick wall. When we get such vibrations, there will be many interesting uses for them. One, at all events would be the possibility of communicating between lightships and the shore.[1]

Trotter had worked as an electric lighting consultant for the Royal Engineers and the Royal Navy during the 1880s. He appreciated the analogy between a signalling lamp and a generator of 'Hertzian' electromagnetic waves. Other people with different education and experience might not make the same connection. The implementation of his idea depended on the attitudes of those responsible for the nation's telegraph system.

An innovation had a reasonable chance of being adopted by the Post Office if it contributed to government communications. But this Civil Service department might not regard better coastal telegraphy as a matter of such high priority. Extra investment, it appeared, would benefit merely the private shipowners and their employees. Only when these shipowners and seamen demonstrated – through the good offices of the RNLI – that they could command political power, was there any real consideration of the means whereby offshore communications might be improved.

Post Office attitudes to technical innovation

By 1891, the Post Office telegraph service and its predecessor, the Electric Telegraph Company, had been in existence for nearly half a century. The time was not propitious for the consideration of new ideas. Large monopolies, established for several decades, often display a marked reluctance to accept innovations originating outside their own organisation. Such ingrained conservatism in the Post Office was reinforced by the strong family traditions within the telegraph industry. Charles Wheatstone was a founder of the British telegraph industry; his nephews, Arthur and Oliver Heaviside, and his son-in-law Robert Sabine were all employed as telegraph engineers. Edwin Clark, the Electric Telegraph Company's first chief engineer, was succeeded by his brother Latimer, and their brother-in-law, William Preece, later held the same position in the Post Office. John Muirhead, formerly a Company employee, set up in business as a manufacturer of telegraph instruments. He later took his two sons, John and Alexander, into the business as managers and, in Alexander's case, as scientific adviser. This relatively small group, interconnected by family and business relationships, dominated Britain's inland telegraphs until the end of the nineteenth century. It was questionable whether any idea originating outside this close community would be greeted with much enthusiasm.

Trotter's suggested marine wireless telegraph in 1891 would not be regarded more favourably than Bell's newly-invented telephone had been in 1877. Graves – then engineer-in-chief, and a former Electric Telegraph Company employee – made it obvious that he was unimpressed by Bell's invention. Writing in a departmental memorandum, he said: '... that I think it to the interest of the Department to hold aloof from him altogether ... many private renters may be inclined to desire the provisions of a telephone in the first instance but afterwards to wish for its replacement by an ordinary instrument.'[2] As late as February 1878, the Postmaster General believed the telephone would appeal only to the renters of private wires.

He saw it, for example, as a means of communicating between different offices and workshops. But the first telephone *exchange* had by then gone into operation in the USA; the technical possibility of interconnecting many subscribers through a nationwide telephone network had already been demonstrated. The Post Office staff may not have troubled to inform themselves of technical developments on the other side of the Atlantic. Perhaps (as seems more likely) they knew of this development but did not appreciate its significance. But in 1879, the first telephone exchange was opened in London. The civil servants realised, at last, that the telephone would offer real competition to the government's telegraphs. Accordingly, the Post Office sued the private companies for infringement of the State's monopoly. Mr Justice Stevens, who heard the case in 1880, ruled that the telephone was indeed a telegraph as defined by the nationalising legislation. Further development of the telephone system, from 1884 onwards, took place under government licences and, eventually, State ownership.

The telephone was the first new technology to be offered to the nationalised telegraph service. Attitudes revealed in the years 1877–84 determined policies about innovation which the Post Office would later apply to the introduction of radio telegraphy. At first, the senior engineering staff under-estimated the potential of the new device (indeed, Graves' predecessor was not merely ignorant of its principles of working but, surprisingly, was not even aware of his own ignorance, describing another of Bell's inventions – the harmonic telegraph – as a 'telephone' in one of his minutes[3]). They discussed it in terms which showed a measure of contempt for apparatus not devised within their own organisation. But when the State authorities discovered the utility of the new equipment, they made sure that any further developments were under their control. No one in any position of authority objected that State regulation of telephones added further duties to a Department which already lacked finance.

For the technical problems of the nationalised telegraph service were exacerbated by a chronic shortage of money. Frank Scudamore (1823–84), second secretary to the Post Office, had predicted in 1868 that a state-owned telegraph system would be not merely self-supporting, but profitable. A reduction in tariffs, he claimed, would attract so much new traffic as to offset more than the loss on individual messages. In practice, this regular profit did not materialise. Scudamore under-estimated the arrears of maintenance inherited from the private telegraph companies and made no proper allowance for increased operating costs accompanying any substantial rise in traffic.[4] The financial record of the nationalised telegraph service over the last three decades of the nineteenth century is given in Table 4.1. It shows how the expected profit was replaced by a steadily-accumulating loss as the traffic increased.

Table 4.1 *Telegraph finances, 1870–1901*

	Number of messages (millions)	Gross receipts (£ million)	Expenditure as % of gross receipts	Annual revenue
1870–71	9.85	0.80	58%	£388,500 profit
1885–86	39.15	1.79	103%	£ 45,137 loss
1900–01	89.58	3.46	110%	£651,881 loss

Source: Garcke, *Telegraphy*, p. 527.

From its early years, the Post Office telegraph service was embarrassed by this lack of finance. Scudamore's misguided attempt to mask the deficit in 1872–73 with funds from the Post Office Savings Bank only made things worse. His action merely drew attention to the problem by prompting a Parliamentary discussion of his conduct. Scudamore was allowed to resign without formal censure. Memories of the unwelcome publicity, however, aggravated the understandable financial caution applied to all Post Office telegraphic transactions. When Graves was asked in 1877 whether the Post Office should negotiate for the exclusive use in Britain of Bell's telephone, he ruled: 'If we do so ... we must get some decided advantage for our assistance. Otherwise ... we set a precedent which will ultimately very much embarrass us.'[5] Official policy was thus defined: the Post Office should not act as a direct or indirect source of finance to assist inventors in developing new telegraphic equipment. The only exceptions would be for such apparatus as was of immediate benefit to the existing Post Office system. This would almost always exclude any thoroughly novel device, such as the telephone or the radio telegraph. It would favour developments of existing apparatus as might be devised by employees or ex-employees of the Post Office service. Other government departments, and especially the Treasury, approved this policy; it invested money only where it brought a prompt financial return in the Department's accounts. Those who would suffer most from this ruling were 'outsider' inventors, with devices not envisaged by the Post Office staff. But they lacked the influence necessary to get the policy modified.

Inadequate appreciation of electromagnetic theory

Preece was promoted to Engineer-in-Chief and Electrician in 1892.[6] He then became responsible for development of a practical marine wireless telegraph, as required for communication with lighthouses and lightships. Forty years of experience since joining the Electric Telegraph Company combined with his status as the Clarks' brother-in-law to inculcate safe, though not always unexciting, habits of conventional practice. Harry Kempe, for many years his principal personal assistant in the Post Office, described him in such phrases as 'not an expert mathematician', 'perpetually and systematically at work', 'would take but four or five hours of sleep', 'ambitious of fame', and as a 'strong personality overcoming numerous official obstacles'.[7] These were the traits of an engineer whose knowledge depended on industriousness and practical experience rather than theoretical study. He was party, as Graves' deputy, to the discussions about technological innovation between 1877 and 1884. It was unlikely that the conservatively-minded Preece would make any significant modification of accepted policy about outsiders' inventions.

Preece was not averse to innovation as such. He had devised the ingenious wireless telegraph across the Solent in 1882, supervised experiments with the inductive wireless system at Lavernock ten years later, and made the first quantitative measurements of the performance of telephone lines in 1885–87. He tried to describe the Post Office's inductive telegraph in terms of the electromagnetic theory used in Hertz's experiments. In 1892, he told a reporter from *The Times*:

The principle underlying this method of communication is precisely analogous to that which governs the transmission of light itself ... The researches of modern physicists have led them to the conclusion that, as light is an effect produced by a succession of exceedingly small waves in the generally pevading ether, so electricity is an effect of the succession of larger waves in the same ether.[8]

It is evident in retrospect, however, that the performance of the wireless telegraph tested that year at Lavernock could be explained completely by mutual induction between the transmitting and receiving wires. Any electromagnetic radiation involved would have been so slight as to have no practical effect.

Nevertheless, Preece could have learned the truth, and consequently have provided a better description of the inductive system, even in 1892. Several physicists were then studying the implications of Clerk Maxwell's electromagnetic theory. But Preece did not seek their help, and evidently thought it unnecessary.

Indeed, he had already rejected the advice of two of the country's leading exponents of Maxwell's theory. After his studies of propagation along telephone lines in the 1880s he summarised his results in an empirical formula:[9]

... the distance-limit of speaking by telephone upon a telegraph wire is not very great. It depends upon the product of the resistance of the circuit (in ohms) R, and the capacity of the circuit (in microfarads) K, or KR. The following figures show approximately the KR which limits easy and practical speech, and indicate the telephonic value of the conductors:

Copper Wire (open)	KR	10,000
Cable or Underground lines	"	8,000
Iron Wire (open)	"	5,000

Preece derived this rule by analogy with a similar formula, published thirty years earlier, for the limiting speeds of signalling over submarine cables.[10] By the mid-1880s, however, physicists had re-considered this problem to allow for the effects of self-inductance. Oliver Heaviside[11] published a mathematical analysis of the propagation of waves along lines in 1887.[12] He deduced from his analysis that adding extra inductance to a telephone line, in the form of loading coils, could be beneficial. Preece did not agree and set out his own analysis in the *Journal of the Society of Telegraph Engineers*.[13] This supported the official Post Office policy. Inductance in a line, Preece said, was generally undesirable, its actual effects were usually so small as to be negligible, and any artificial increase in its value (as, for instance, by adding loading coils) could only be harmful.

There need have been nothing destructive about this dispute. On the contrary, such argument is an understood part of the process whereby a new theory gains general acceptance. Preece, however, went further. As Hunt has shown,[14] he used his position within the Post Office hierarchy to suppress Heaviside's own contribution to the *Journal of the Society of Telegraph Engineers*. Hunt also suggests that Preece may have imposed a similar censorship on *The Electrician*.

At any rate, its editor, C. H. W. Biggs, resigned in October 1887 and his successor, W. H. Snell, refused to publish Heaviside's articles. Preece had, temporarily, brought the debate to an end — but without convincing his opponents that his own opinion was correct.

Within a year, Preece was involved in a second dispute about the practical application of contemporary electromagnetic theory. This time his opponent was Oliver Lodge,[15] then Professor of Experimental Physics at University College, Liverpool. Lodge published the results of his experiments with lightning conductors in the Mann lectures to the Society of Arts on 10 March and 17 March 1888. His findings were controversial, being in some respects contrary to the recommendations of the British Association's Lightning Rod Conference. Lodge claimed to show that: '... an electric discharge was not a simple rush in one direction along a single path whose property depended only on its conductance, but that the best conductor offered considerable opposition, so that when struck by a flash it did not convey the flash easily to the ground ... because of its inductance'.[16] Here again, the effects of inductance appeared contrary to practical experience!

The British Association recognised the publicity value of an academic argument. They arranged for a debate on lightning protection at their meeting that September in Bath. Lodge opened the discussion. He claimed that a lightning conductor designed solely to meet the Lightning Rod Conference criterion of low resistance could, by its inductance, impose considerable impedance to an oscillatory discharge. Preece, having been Secretary of the Lightning Rod Conference, was chosen to defend their recommendations. He said that inductive effects, if any, would be so small as to be negligible.

Preece based his argument on years of practical experience within the Post Office and similar organisations. This was a wise decision from Preece's point of view. It appealled to practical engineers who were not trained to understand Lodge's mathematical abstractions. As a former President of the Society of Telegraph Engineers (1881) and Engineer-in-Chief to the Post Office, Preece spoke from a position of considerable authority; Lodge was a relatively young professor from one of the new provincial colleges. The more practically-oriented technical journals considered that Preece had the better of these exchanges. One published a cartoon showing Preece as a gladiator standing victorious over his fallen rival, Lodge. Preece held a lightning-conductor as a spear, bearing a pennant labelled

'Experience', while Lodge was likewise armed to defend 'Experiment'. The cartoonist evidently believed that the debate had wider implications than a mere discussion of a point of technical practice. But the practising engineers were not the only people to perceive these wider issues. Lodge had his supporters, too. Heaviside wrote to the editor of *The Electrician* about the dispute at the British Association, observing sarcastically: '... although Mr Preece, who as a practical engineer, knows all about electromagnetic inertia and throttling, does not see the use of inductance, impedance and all that sort of thing, yet there is not wanting evidence to make it not wholly unbelievable that Mr Preece is not fully acquainted with the subject'.[17] Other well-known physicists, including Kelvin, Thompson and Carey Foster, though less belligerent, recorded their agreement with Lodge.

Electricians and applied scientists

By the end of 1892, the campaign for the improvement of Britain's offshore communications appeared to have achieved all its aims. There was State finance, assured by a unanimous vote in the House of Commons; there was State support for the research, to be exercised through the Post Office; there was the necessary scientific knowledge, as indicated by Trotter. It was, however, questionable whether the Post Office engineering department was the most effective catalyst for combining these elements into a useful wireless telegraph. Preece, their engineer-in-chief, may or may not have been aware of Trotter's suggestion to use electromagnetic radiation for signalling in 1891. But one thing is certain. He was no more willing to accept electromagnetic theory into Post Office techniques than he was to accept other ideas originating outside his department. Heaviside, one of his antagonists had a very short career as a telegrapher and no academic qualifications, it is true. Moreover, instead of presenting his findings in a diplomatic fashion, Heaviside had adopted the sarcastic manner for which he was already notorious.[18] All the same, Preece was responsible for ensuring that his department was aware of anything which might affect current technology. He should not have dismissed so lightly a topic which had aroused the interest of several well-known scientists. Most certainly, he should not have misused his position in an attempt to suppress all discussion of the subject.

Yet Preece's behaviour is understandable. Like most telegraph engineers of his generation, he had received his training at a time when many believed, in the words of a contemporary technical journal, that '... in electricity there is seldom any need of mathematical or other abstractions ...'.[19] He claimed that he had later learned to respect the importance of theoretical study. But the continued opposition of Heaviside and Lodge released his underlying prejudices. He spoke scornfully at the Institution of Electrical Engineers in 1893 about such '... visionary mathematicians who monopolise the columns of our technical literature, scorning the practical man and scoffing at his experience'.[20] Preece was unused to criticism of his own technical knowledge; he had been Electrician to the Post Office for more than a decade, with no superior to question his judgements. Indeed, his position in the Civil Service was unassailable. When it was pointed out in Parliament in 1892 that his extensive private consultancy was a flagrant breach of his own department's rules, the official government response was simply that 'the case of Mr Preece is exceptional'.[21] It was little wonder, then, that he developed what Tucker has described[22] as an 'arrogant self-confidence which led him into serious error on occasions'.

Preece was typical of those leaders of British industry who failed to appreciate contemporary science. But such attitudes were not peculiar to Britain. In fact, they were also evident among the industrialists of some of Britain's main competitors. The famous Edison dismissed one of his assistants, Nikola Tesla,[23] after a succession of technical quarrels. These involved, among other topics, the relative merits of the novel alternating-current power distribution systems that Tesla proposed, and the simpler direct-current apparatus which Edison was already using. Here again, a basic cause of disagreement was the inability of the self-educated Edison to understand the mathematical and physical principles which Tesla, a university graduate, used in his designs. In consequence, Charles Westinghouse was able to purchase the Tesla patents and develop an alternating-current system. Significantly, the engineer employed by Westinghouse in 1888 to investigate Tesla's proposals admitted that he could not then understand the principles of operation of the alternating-current induction motor, although he was convinced of its utility by the simple fact of seeing one in operation.[24]

Electrical engineering – and telegraphy in particular – was in a state of transition. Self-taught 'electricians', relying on practical experience as their principal source of information, were still in control of the industry. But in 1892, when Preece was promoted to head the Post Office's engineering service, a new generation of mathematically − trained applied scientists was attaining positions of influence. Trotter, thirty-five years old, was a technical journalist, while Tesla, at thirty-six, was a consultant; both were university science graduates. The thirty-seven year old Jackson was on the staff of a naval technical school, Lodge, slightly older at forty-one, was a professor in a provincial University College. The new scientific methods introduced by this younger generation of applied scientists were not welcomed by the industry's leaders. Indeed the editor of *The Engineer* went so far as to declare that '... the world owes next to nothing to the man of pure science ... the engineer, and the engineer alone, is the great civilizer. The man of science follows in his train.'[25] Preece was scarcely less restrained when he wrote to Lodge that '... I cannot recall to mind one single instance where I have derived any benefit from pure theory'.[26]

The mathematically-trained applied scientists were not yet occupying posts of high public authority. Yet they had been the first to recognise the weaknesses in the Empire's communications system. And they did most to correct these weaknesses. Jackson and his colleagues in the Royal Navy had identified the need for a better means of marine telegraphy. Trotter (though considering the requirements of the merchant service rather than the Royal Navy) realised that Hertzian electromagnetic radiation might be adapted to meet this need. He published this idea in the technical press, adding a practical comment to theoretical studies by Hertz, Heaviside, Lodge and Tesla. And experience would show that these applied scientists would eventually provide the efficient wireless telegraph which the Empire needed. Heaviside, Lodge and Jackson would add their own contributions to the work of such foreign physicists as Hertz and Tesla to produce a practical radio system.

References

1 A.P. Trotter, *The Electrician*, XXVI, 1891, pp. 685−6.
2 K. Geddes, 'The GPO and the Telephone, 1877−1879', *Papers Presented at the Third IEE Weekend Meeting on the History of Electrical Engineering*, 1975, p. 11/2.
3 Geddes, *The GPO and the Telephone*, p. 11/1.
4 J.L. Kieve, *The Electric Telegraph: a Social and Economic History*, Newton Abbot, David & Charles, 1973, pp. 178−9.
5 Geddes, *The GPO and the Telephone*, p. 11/2.

6   Preece's official title in 1877 had been Deputy Engineer-in-Chief and Electrician to identify his particular area of responsibility. He retained the latter part of this title, at his own request, after Graves's death in 1892.

7   D.G. Tucker, 'Sir William Preece (1834–1913)', *Transactions of the Newcomen Society*, LIII, 1982, pp. 119–20.

8   *The Times*, 22 November 1892.

9   W.H. Preece and J. Sivewright, *Telegraphy*, London, Longmans Green, 1891, p. 236.

10   W. Thompson, 'On the theory of the electric telegraph', *Proc. R. Soc.*, VII, 1855, pp. 382–99.

11   Oliver Heaviside, FRS (1850–1924). Wheatstone's nephew, was employed as a telegraph operator by the Great Northern company, but retired in 1874 and thereafter lived very frugally on a limited private income, devoting his time to the study of mathematics and mathematical physics.

12   O. Heaviside, *Electrical Papers*, London, Macmillan, 1892, pp. 223–54.

13   W.H. Preece, 'The limiting distance of speech by telephone', *J. Soc. Teleg. Eng.*, XVI, 1887, pp. 265–8.

14   B.J. Hunt, 'Practice vs theory: the British electrical debate, 1888–1891', *Isis*, LXXIV, 1983, pp. 347–8.

15   Later Sir Oliver Lodge, FRS (1851–1940), Professor of Experimental Physics, University College, Liverpool, 1881–1900; first Principal of the University of Birmingham 1900–19.

16   O.J. Lodge, *Advancing Science*, London, Benn, 1931, p. 95.

17   O. Heaviside, 'Practice vs theory – electromagnetic waves', *The Electrician*, XXI, 1888, p. 772.

18   G. Lee, 'Oliver Heaviside – the man', *The Heaviside Centenary Volume*, London, The Institution of Electrical Engineers, 1950, p. 11.

19   W. Jackson, 'An appreciation of Heaviside's contribution to electromagnetic theory', *Heaviside Centenary Volume*, p. 53.

20   E.C. Baker, *Sir William Preece, FRS: Victorian Engineer Extraordinary*, London, Hutchinson, p. 211.

21   Tucker, *Sir William Preece*, p. 131.

22   *Ibid*, p. 120.

23   Nikola Tesla (1856–1943), Serbian-born, educated at the Gratz technical college and the University of Prague. Emigrated to the USA in 1884 where, after a short period as Edison's assistant and subsequently as a general labourer, he founded the Tesla Electric Company in 1887. Offered, but refused, the Nobel Prize for Physics in 1912.

24   H.C. Passer, *The Electrical Manufacturers, 1875–1900*, Cambridge, Mass., Harvard University Press, 1953, pp. 277–8.

25   Anon, 'Next to nothing', *The Engineer*, LXVI, 1888, p. 203.

26   Hunt, *Practice vs Theory*, p. 349.

PART II
Science and social reform

Chart of principal events, 1890–1896

	Hertz/Lodge/Jackson	Marconi	Branly/Popov	Publications
1890	Lodge introduces improved transmitter		Branly discovers principle of coherer	
1891				Trotter's suggestion of radio in *The Electrician*
1892				Crookes' prophetic article in the *Fortnightly Review*
1893				Tesla's suggestion for radio in *J. Franklin Inst.*
1894 Jan	Death of Hertz			English translation of Hertz's *Electric Waves*
Feb				
Mar				
Apr				Righi's obituary of Hertz in *Il Nuovo Cimento*
May				
Jun				
Jul				
Aug	Lodge demonstrates Morse signalling to the British Association at Oxford			
Sep				
Oct		Start of Marconi's experiments at Bologna		
Nov				Lodge's book *The Work of Hertz & His Successors*
Dec				

	Jackson	Marconi	Popov / Publications
1895			
Jan			
Feb			
Mar			
Apr			
May			Popov's lightning detector in operation
Jun		Marconi's outdoor experiments	
Jul			
Aug			
Sep			
Oct			
Nov			
Dec	Start of Jackson's experiments in HMS *Defiance*		
1896			
Jan			
Feb		Marconi emigrates to Britain	Editorial article about radio in *The Electrician*
Mar			Popov demonstrates Morse signalling
Apr		Marconi contacts G.P.O. and War Office	
May			
Jun		Marconi's provisional patent filed	
Jul			
Aug	Jackson demonstrates Morse signalling — Meeting of Jackson and Marconi at War Office —		
Sep			First published account of Marconi's work in *The Times*

5

The outsiders' contributions

... Hertz's experiment proves the ethereal theory.

G.F. Fitzgerald, 1888

By the 1890s, public opinion − or, at any rate, that influential part of it which found expression through Parliament and the press − acknowledged the need for an effective wireless telegraph as part of the nation's coastal communications. It also accepted that the country's applied scientists were responsible for developing the devices to meet this need.

In the manner of other Victorian middle-class professionals, the scientists and engineers involved in electrical studies had organised themselves into a learned society. Their representative body, the Society of Telegraph Engineers, was founded in May 1871. Despite its title, the Society concerned itself with all applications of electricity and did not restrict its membership to telegraphers. As electric power, traction and lighting became more important, its title was changed to the Society of Telegraph Engineers and Electricians in 1880 and then again to the Institution of Electrical Engineers in 1889. With several influential civil servants such as Scudamore and Preece among its founders, there was a strong incentive for their subordinates to join. An analysis of members' occupations during these early years shows that the Post Office's telegraphers dominated the new Society.[1]

GPO and army telegraphs	60%
Academic science	19%
Railway and foreign telegraphs	15%
Manufacture	6%

Naval officers, like Jackson, were generally admitted only as Associates, though Colomb, the naval signals expert, was one of the Society's founders.

Most of the members had been, in the words of the Society's regulations: '... regularly educated as a Telegraph Engineer, according to the usual routine of pupilage, and ... had subsequent employment for at least five years in responsible situations', or else had '... practised ... in the profession of a Telegraph Engineer for at least two years, and ... acquired a degree of eminence in the same'. The emphasis was therefore on practical experience rather than on any kind of formal scientific education, although some members in the public service (including Tyndall, Playfair and Fleeming Jenkin) had graduated from the science faculties of Continental universities. The aristocrats of the Society were such eminent mathematical physicists as Maxwell and Kelvin, who had been offered membership because of their contributions to electrical theory. Some were aristocrats in a social as well as in a professional sense: Maxwell, for instance, was of the Scottish nobility, and Kelvin was elevated to the peerage in 1892. Their positions in society were recognition of their researches in pure physics, and did not depend on practical applications of their work (Kelvin's improvements in navigating instruments, for instance, were regarded as an outcome of his hobby – yachting).

Most of these mathematical physicists had qualified by passing the examinations of the Cambridge mathematical tripos. The high quality of mathematics teaching at the University, renowned since Newton's time, was reinforced by the social standing of the individual graduates and the status then associated with the study of pure rather than applied science. They were a small, coherent elite which dominated British (and, to some extent, European) physics during the later nineteenth century. Their University's influence was further extended into nearly every important establishment for scientific education by Cambridge graduates appointed to teaching posts in public schools and technical colleges.[2]

Contributions to the study of electromagnetic radiation

Maxwell published his electromagnetic theory in 1864. This theory was the basis of radio telegraphy; it was also the last important contribution from Cambridge mathematical physicists to the development of radio during the nineteenth century. As originally formulated, the theory showed that visible light had the properties of an electromagnetic wave in an all-pervading aether. It also implied, but did not state explicitly, that there might be similar, but invisible radiations of a hitherto unsuspected kind. Chalmers's study suggests that Maxwell himself did not appreciate this implicit possibility.[3] Between 1871 and 1879, four reliable investigators observed phenomena which can now be recognised as manifestations of this invisible radiation.[4] Three of these investigators described their observations in reputable scientific journals, but no one realised at the time that they were providing experimental confirmation of Maxwell's deductions.

In 1880, G.F. Fitzgerald – of Trinity College, Dublin – published the first of three papers which investigated the possibility of generating invisible electromagnetic waves.[5] Evidently even Fitzgerald had his doubts about the existence of such waves. Lodge later revealed that his paper was originally entitled 'On the Impossibility of Originating Wave Disturbances in the Ether by Electromagnetic Forces', the first syllable of the third word being subsequently deleted.[6] By 1883, however, these doubts had been resolved and Fitzgerald presented two further papers[7] to the British Association which described theoretically how such radiation might be generated: '... utilising the alternating currents produced when an accumulator [a capacitor, in modern terminology] is discharged through a small resistance. It would·be possible to produce waves of as little as 10 metres wavelength, or even less.'

These early papers about electromagnetic radiation emphasised the generation of short, high-frequency waves. These would have properties similar to the very short wavelengths of visible light. Pure scientists were interested in the similarities between invisible radiations and visible light. Applied scientists would later find the differences in their properties, such as the ability to penetrate fog, more important.

The next major development of electromagnetic theory was due to Heaviside, one of these applied scientists. As a retired telegraph engineer, he was interested in phenomena associated with conductors rather than the same phenomena in free space. Following Maxwell's example, he abandoned traditional methods of considering telegraph circuits in terms of charge and current, instead describing their behaviour in relation to the associated electrical and magnetic fields. But he re-cast Maxwell's formulae to deal with measurable electrical and magnetic forces rather than the immeasurable vector potential and scalar potential preferred by mathematical physicists. He published a full explanation of these changes in 1885,[8] though some of his methods had been introduced in earlier papers.

Heaviside did more than simply translate Maxwell's theories.

His papers in *The Electrician* made those theories accessible to practically-oriented engineers and applied scientists who might otherwise have ignored their implications. Some electricians – Preece, for instance – were not willing to accept the consequences of his work. Those with adequate mathematical knowledge welcomed his contribution. Fitzgerald, in reviewing Heaviside's papers, remarked that:

Maxwell, like every other pioneer who does not live to explore the country he opened out, had not had time to investigate the most direct means of access to the country nor the most systematic way of exploring it. This has been reserved for Oliver Heaviside to do ... The maze of symbols, electric and magnetic potential, vector potential, electric force, current displacement, magnetic force and induction, have been practically reduced to two, electric and magnetic force.[9]

It was not only in his native Britain that Heaviside's work had such a favourable reception. Hertz wrote to him from Karlsruhe that 'You have gone further on than Maxwell ... if he lived, he would have acknowledged the superiority of your methods.'[10] Nearly two decades later Lorentz, the Professor of Physics at Leiden University, expressed similar opinions. He said that students should not use Maxwell's equations 'in the rather complex form in which they can be found in Maxwell's treatise, but in the clearer and more condensed form that has been given them by Heaviside and Hertz'.[11]

Hertz took the theoretical work of Fitzgerald and Heaviside to its logical conclusion, actually generating and measuring invisible electromagnetic radiation. A student of mechanical engineering, Hertz eventually made a career in pure science. After studying under Herman von Helmholtz in Berlin, he was appointed Professor of Physics at Karlsruhe. It was there, in 1885, that he started his studies in electromagnetic theory.

Maxwell's theory was then regarded by German physicists as but one of several hypotheses concerning electrical and magnetic induction. Indeed, the 'positivist' approach of German physicists of what is sometimes called the 'action-at-a-distance' school, taking account in theory only of those phenomena which could be attested by observation and measurement, attempted to interpret electromagnetism without resorting to abstract concepts such as the displacement currents in an imponderable aether, which were an essential part of Maxwell's electrodynamics. An open-ended circuit (a radio aerial, in modern terminology) provided a way of comparing these two approaches to electrical studies. If such a circuit were a complete system in itself, then the principle of conservation of energy implied that it should not radiate. But according to Maxwell's theory, the circuit should be closed by displacement currents in the aether. Energy could, in that case, be transferred from the circuit to the aether and, as Fitzgerald suggested, radiated into space.

Hertz's first results, published on 10 November 1887, were inconsistent. But they showed that Fitzgerald was correct in predicting that an open-ended oscillating circuit would radiate and that Maxwell had been right when he asserted that electromagnetic effects were propagated with finite velocity. The oscillating circuit was a Leyden jar (Fitzgerald's 'accumulator') discharging through a coil; the detector was a simple loop of wire which lay nearby. Hertz noticed that when the jar was discharged, a small spark passed across a gap in the wire loop. Energy was radiated from the coil to the loop, and reached one end of the loop a short time before the other. Consequently a potential difference existed across the gap. Having demonstrated that electromagnetic radiation existed, Hertz devoted much of his time in 1888−89 to an investigation of its properties. His findings, in five successive papers, established that this newly-discovered radiation was indeed similar to visible light.[12]

Only four months after the publication of Hertz's discoveries, Lodge detected similar electromagnetic waves on metallic wires. He generated these waves during his controversial experiments with lightning conductors; using the discharge of a Leyden jar to simulate a lightning flash, he had virtually the same transmitter as Hertz. Describing his experiments to the British Association in September 1888, Lodge explained that the oscillating currents when the Leyden jar discharged 'disturb the surrounding medium and send out radiation of the precise nature of light'.[12] Further, he showed how the constants of the guiding wires could be adjusted to bring them into resonance with the jar's circuits − 'tuning' the system, in modern terminology. A postscript to his printed paper drew attention to the recently-published work of Hertz:

wherein he establishes the existence and measures the length of aether waves excited by coil discharges; converting them into stationary waves, not by reflexion of pulses transmitted along a wire and reflected at its free end, as I have done, but by reflexion of waves in free space at the surface of a conducting wall ... The whole subject of electric radiation seems working itself out splendidly.

The impressive experiments by Hertz, together with the publicity about the lightning-conductor dispute, received more coverage than Lodge's paper did in the technical press. But Heaviside, among others, understood what had been accomplished. He wrote that 'to an unbiased mind the experiments of Prof. Lodge, sending waves of short length into a miniature telegraph circuit, with consequent "resonance" effects, are equally conclusive to those of Hertz'.[14]

The applied scientists who had deduced and demonstrated the existence of electromagnetic radiation — and thereby established the scientific basis of radio telegraphy — were neither practical telegraphers nor Cambridge-educated mathematical physicists. Heaviside was the only telegraph engineer among them, and his short term of employment did not qualify him for anything better than Associate membership of the Society of Telegraph Engineers. None of these applied scientists was a physics graduate from a Continental university. Lodge had not even received a full-time university education, but had qualified (as had Muirhead) after study at various technical colleges by passing the University of London's examinations. Whatever the actual attitudes of their fellow-members, they considered themselves 'outsiders' among the practical electricians and pure scientists of the Institution of Electrical Engineers. Even William Crookes,[15] although he was the Institution's President in 1891, complained that lack of what he called a 'university gown' hindered his acceptance as an equal among academic scientists.[16] Crookes had been educated at the State-controlled Royal College of Chemistry, which was not then a degree-awarding institution. Heaviside felt much the same as Crookes, and complained after an editor's rejection of one of his mathematical papers that 'even men who are not Cambridge mathematicians deserve justice: which I fear they do not always get'.[17] Lodge, too, observed later in life that:

I believe that my real line would have been mathematical physics, if I had had the necessary training all through those receptive years from the age of fifteen to twenty-two; but it was not until I was twenty-three that I began the serious study of higher mathematics, and even then never went through the Cambridge course.

I always regretted that I didn't go through the Cambridge grind, for I am thus somewhat isolated from those who did. It is a very wonderful system that is carried on at Cambridge, and they had great teachers there.[18]

Despite their own contributions to applied science, Heaviside and Lodge evidently aspired to the status of the pure scientists educated at Cambridge and not to that of the scientists in the government service who, like Tyndall of the Board of Trade, had graduated from German or Italian universities. The same was true of Crookes, who, according to de Kosky, 'had a burning desire for fundamental discovery and consequent eminence'.[19] This ambition to achieve recognition in pure rather than applied science may be an example of the attitudes identified by Wiener as resulting from anti-industrial cultural values. But such attitudes were not confined to British scientists; Hertz changed from a career in engineering to one in mathematical physics, but nevertheless felt an 'outsider' among German academic scientists. He told Lodge 'of the difficulty he had in getting his ideas accepted in Germany, where the professors ... did not understand Maxwell'.[20] (Indeed, had Heaviside and Lodge enjoyed the German scientific education received by some of their contemporaries, their researches might well have been inhibited by the teachings of 'action-at-a-distance' physics.)

Even Tesla, although working in the technology-conscious USA, aspired to a career in pure science. He was described by his friend O'Neill as making 'a very definite distinction between the inventor of useful appliances and the discoverer of new principles',[21] and as regarding himself in the latter category. Tesla's argument with the telegraph electricians in the New World enhanced his sympathy for Heaviside and Lodge during their similar debates with Preece. He was later to express admiration for the work of Lodge and, especially, of Crookes.

A common sense of isolation and unfulfilled ambition linked these individual applied scientists. They were all from lower middle-class families – Crookes's, Heaviside's and Lodge's fathers ran successful businesses, while Tesla was the son of a Serbian orthodox priest – and their educations, while providing the advanced mathematical theory which Preece and the electricians lacked, emphasised the practical orientation of technical colleges instead of the science faculties of universities in Britain or on the Continent. By the 1890s, when their contributions to electromagnetic theory were recognised, they had formed an identifiable group that maintained its cohesion by informal meetings and by correspondence.

Improvements in transmitters and receivers

While mathematical physicists and electricians alike were still considering the implications of Hertz's discoveries, the applied scientists actually involved in electromagnetic wave research were improving their experimental techniques. Neither Hertz nor Lodge used very sophisticated apparatus in their early experiments. They generated radiation by discharging Leyden jars and detected this radiation by observing small sparks in a tuned loop. The transmitter produced only a single, rapidly-damped pulse of radiation; the detector involved an unacceptable degree of subjective judgement.

Hertz soon replaced the Leyden jar in his transmitter with an induction coil which produced a train of pulses. With the secondary spark-gap of the coil at the focus of a parabolic reflector, this generator provided a narrow pencil of radiation. The secondary circuits were charged to a high voltage, and were discharged when a spark passed between the secondary terminals. Electromagnetic waves, at a frequency of about 40 MHz, were generated by the resulting oscillatory currents in the secondary circuit. Lodge later modified the simple Hertzian arrangement by introducing further metal spheres between the secondary terminals, making several spark-gaps in series. He claimed that the electrical constants of this circuit were determined by the dimensions of the metal spheres, so that it generated a wave of constant frequency.[22]

Edouard Branly (1846–1940), a French physicist, was responsible for an even more fundamental improvement in the detector circuits. He observed in 1890 that the resistance of a glass tube packed with metal filings fell sharply when near an operating electostatic generator.[23] This effect was more rapidly detected and more easily incorporated in a circuit for quantitative measurement than Hertz's secondary spark. Branly's filings-tube was the most popular detector of electromagnetic radiation for the rest of the nineteenth century. Its usual name, the 'coherer', was introduced by Lodge in 1894.

Fitzgerald in Ireland, and Heaviside in Britain, had re-formulated Maxwell's theory in terms which were a useful basis for the study of electromagnetic waves. Hertz in Germany, Lodge in Britain, and Branly in France had designed apparatus to generate and detect these waves. Details of their work were published in European technical journals and disseminated in the USA through a series of lectures by Tesla. As Trotter recognised in 1891, all the essential elements of a wireless telegraph suitable for use in lighthouses and lightships existed and had been discribed in the press. But the scientists involved were not trying to produce a new telegraph system (Heaviside's and Lodge's practical studies were confined to a better understanding of the theoretical principles determining the behaviour of existing devices). The attitudes of most physicists were summarised by Fitzgerald's Presidential Address to Section A of the British Association at its historic Bath meeting in September 1888. Contemporary conflicting physical theories had, Fitzgerald said:

been experimentally decided by Hertz in Germany ... in favour of the hypothesis that actions take place by means of an intervening medium ... Hertz's experiment proves the ethereal theory of electro-magnetism ... Fire, water, earth and air have long been his slaves, but it is only within the last few years that man has won the battle lost by the giants of old, has snatched the thunderbolt from Jove himself and enslaved the all-pervading ether.[24]

The aether in pure and applied physics

This all-pervading aether which, Fitzgerald claimed, had been revealed by Hertz's experiments, was a major topic of study for nineteenth-century physicists. It had been described by Maxwell in 1865[25] as a 'medium pervading all bodies ... the parts of this medium are capable of being set in motion by electric currents and magnets ... this motion is communicated from one part of the medium to another by forces arising from connexions of the parts'. During the next two decades, aetheric properties were invoked in explanation of various physical phenomena. Its perceived functions were summarised by Lodge as:

... One continuous substance filling all space; which can vibrate as light; which can be sheared into positive and negative electricity; which in whirls constitutes matter; and which transmits by continuity, and not by impact, every action and reaction of which matter is capable.[26]

In other words, the aether was regarded as the basic material from which all matter and all energy were formed.

Mathematical physicists were interested in 'Hertzian' electromagnetic radiation as a tool for the further investigation of the aether. In particular, this radiation might be used for the study of atoms which were then, as Lodge described, believed to be vortices in the aether. The mathematical physicists had little interest in the properties of the electromagnetic waves as such. Only one Cambridge physicist of note experimented along the lines established by Hertz, and he was not from the mainstream of British scientists. Ernest Rutherford (1871–1937), a New Zealander studying at Cambridge on an Exhibition Fellowship, designed a novel detector of Hertzian radiation for his researches in 1895–96.[27] But Rutherford's experiments were not primarily concerned with the waves themselves. He said in January 1896 that he hoped to make 'a considerable amount of money' from an apparatus 'to connect lighthouses and lighships to the shore so that signals could be sent at any time'.[28] But Rutherford did not pursue this application in practice. In fact, he abandoned the research soon afterwards. It was left to Marconi, early in the twentieth century, to develop Rutherford's magnetic detector into a useful substitute for the coherer.[29]

For, during the 1890s, while radio developed into a practical system of telegraphy, physical theory was undergoing a fundemental change. Mathematical physicists were less concerned with interpreting phenomena in terms of an aethereal plenum, but sought explanations instead in the interactions of discrete sub-atomic particles. Applied scientists, on the other hand, looked for means of controlling the electromagnetic radiation which Hertz had discovered, and found Maxwell's electrodynamic theory still to be adequate for their purposes. This dichotomy in the theoretical approach emphasised the division between pure and applied physics. Tesla was interested in possible applications of very high-frequency alternating currents to power transmission systems. Lodge predicted in 1881 that the general adoption of electric power would 'restore our large towns to their old habitable beauty and healthfulness before the smoke-demon blackened the sky'.[30] Both retained a belief in the aether as an essential part of their theoretical studies, and both regarded this aether, the source of all electrical phenomena, as a medium to be exploited for the common good.

But this belief in the existence of an aether was not due solely to theoretical conservatism. They regarded this mysterious imponderable medium as the source of more than material phenomena. Tesla, during a lecture-tour of Europe in 1892, believed that he received a supernatural message from his mother at the instant of her death.[31]- Crookes[32] and Lodge,[33] whom he met during this his tour, likewise thought they had been contacted by deceased relatives. They concluded that such spiritual messages were probably transmitted through the aether. This opinion was consistent with a well-known hypothesis advanced by two Cambridge-educated physicists, Balfour Stewart (1828–87) and Peter Guthrie Tait (1831–1901) in 1874.[34] Stewart and Tait suggested that the aether was a common link between the natural and supernatural Orders. It might, they said, provide a means of intervention by a Divine creator in natural events without violating the principle of conservation of energy. By the 1920s most physicists no longer invoked an aether in their theoretical writings. But Lodge, interested in psychic and metaphysical studies, still considered the aether to be much as Stewart and Tait had described it fifty years earlier. Tesla repudiated any religious belief, but he, too, regarded the existence of an aether as essential to his mechanistic view of human nature. He wrote that 'we are automata entirely controlled by the forces of that medium ... mistaking the resultant of the impulses from outside for free will'.[35]

A common belief in spiritualism further unified the group of applied scientists. It also encouraged their attempts to utilise scientific discoveries for the solution of social problems. The early spiritualist movement (typified by such organisations as the National Association of Spiritualists, founded in 1873) was associated strongly with populist causes and reformist politics. Its followers generally were as concerned with the alleviation of unsatisfactory social conditions on this earth as with the establishment of contacts in the next world. But neither Lodge nor Tesla made any immediate attempt to utilise electromagnetic radiation in a signalling system. They still hoped to be recognised for their discoveries in pure science. Further information about the mysterious aether would have immediate consequences for the developmnt of Maxwell's theory. It might also, in the longer term, provide material to be exploited for the solution of social problems.

Fitzgerald and Lodge investigated what was then considered the most important outstanding problem of aetheric behaviour; whether or not the aether experienced anything comparable with a 'frictional' drag in the vicinity of massive bodies. Experiments by Michelson and Morley in 1887 had detected no relative movement between the earth's surface and the assumed – stationary aether; Fitzgerald suggested that this result was not evidence of aether-drag but of a dilation in the dimensions of measuring instruments moving with the earth – a dilation effect deduced independently by Lorentz at about the same time. Lodge agreed with Fitzgerald's conclusions, and subsequently provided a rigorous confirmation of the Michelson – Morley findings by his own experiments with an elaborate 'aether-machine'. The published paper presenting his results and deductions[36] gained him the Rumford Medal of the Royal Society. This was confirmation that he had achieved the recognition as a mathematical physicist which he had desired for so long.

Studies of the aether in the vicinity of massive bodies led to consideration of the properties of Hertzian waves in the most massive body then accessible to experimenters, the earth itself. Fitzgerald wrote in 1893 that:

The period of oscillation of a simple sphere of the size of the earth, supposed charged with opposite charges of electricity at its ends, would be about 1/17 of a second, but the hypothesis that the earth is a conducting body surrounded by a non-conductor is not in accordance with fact. Probably the upper regions of our atmosphere are fairly good conductors ... If we assume the height of the region of the aurora (ie. the upper conducting layer) to be 60 miles, or 100 kilometres, we get a period of oscillation of 0·1 sec ... Dr Lodge has already looked for evidence ... on the assumption that the period would be 1/17 sec; but with a negative result.[37]

Tesla started experiments in May 1899 at Colorado Springs to generate and detect waves such as Fitzgerald had described. He subsequently claimed to have determined the periodicity of standing waves in the earth's electrostatic charge to be about one-sixth of a second,[38] which would have corresponded, on Fitzgerald's calculation, with a conducting layer in the atmosphere at an altitude of about 100 kilometres. Measurements by Appleton in 1926 confirmed that there was indeed such a layer (the Kennelly − Heaviside layer) at an altitude of between 80 and 120 kilometres.

These aetheric studies were far removed from the problems of everyday life. But they were not inspired solely by a search for knowledge though they involved important long-term considerations for applied science. In the 1930s, Lodge wrote that '... matter has many imperfections, and it is part of our business on this planet to struggle with it and cause it to do what we want.'[39] Tesla likewise claimed that '... to create and to annihilate material substance, cause it to aggregate in forms according to his desire, would be the supreme manifestation of the power of Man's mind, his most complete triumph over the physical world'[40] Both envisaged the mastery of the aether as the means of achieving this ultimate power. Electromagnetic wave researchers seemed to have ignored the immediate requirements of the Royal Navy and of the coastal resuce services.

But events would show that, in the short term, Hertzian wave research was to be applied to the mundane, but nevertheless pressing, need for an efficient wireless telegraph to offset natural hazards like fog and bad weather.

References

1   R. Appleyard, *The History of the Institution of Electrical Engineers 1871–1931*, London, The Institution of Electrical Engineers, 1939, p. 43.

2   D. S. L. Cardwell, *The Organisation of Science in England*, London, Heinemann, 1972, pp. 239–40.

3   A. F. Chalmers, *The Electromagnetic Theory of James Clerk Maxwell*, PhD Thesis, University of London, 1971.

4   Professor Süsskind ('Observations of electromagnetic wave radiation before Hertz', *Isis*, LV, 1964, pp. 32–42) indentifies observations by Thomas Edison (1875), Elihu Thomson (1871), Silvanus P. Thompson (1876) and David Hughes (1879). Hughes missed a great opportunity. He demonstrated his experiments to Stokes and other eminent physicists. But they did not contradict his own belief that his results were due to well-known inductive effects. Consequently, he published no description of the experiments until 1899, when the work of Marconi and other radio engineers had alerted even the popular press to the properties of electromagnetic radiation!

5   G. F. Fitzgerald, 'On the possibility of originating wave disturbances in the ether by electromagnetic forces', *Sci. Trans Royal Dublin Soc.*, I, 1880, pp. 133–4 and 173–6.

6   O. J. Lodge, *Advancing Science*, London, Benn, 1931, p. 55.

7   G. F. Fitzgerald, 'On a method of producing electromagnetic disturbances of comparatively short wavelengths', *Brit. Assoc. Report*, LIII, 1883, p. 405; 'On the energy lost by radiation from alternating currents', *Sci, Trans. Royal Dublin Society*, III, 1883, pp. 57–60.

8   O. Heaviside, 'Electromagnetic induction and its propagation', *The Electrician*, XIV, 1885, p. 148.

9   G. F. Fitzgerald, *The Electrician*, XXXI, 1893, p. 389.

10   W. Jackson, 'An appreciation of Heaviside's contribution to electromagnetic theory', *The Heaviside Centenary Volume*, London, The Institution of Electrical Engineers, 1950, pp. 56–7.

11   Jackson, *'Heaviside's contribution'*, p. 57.

12   H. Hertz, *Untersuchungen uber die Ausbreitung der elektrischen Kraft*, Leipzig, Johann Ambrosius Barth, 1892.

13   O. J. Lodge, 'On the theory of lightning conductors', *Philos, Mag.*, XXVI, 1888, pp. 217–30.

14   O. Heaviside, *Electrical Papers*, London, Macmillan, p. 489.

15   Sir William Crookes (1832–1919), scientific journalist and consultant. President of the Institution of Electrical Engineers, 1891; President of the British Association, 1898; President of the Society for Psychic Research, 1897; President of the Royal Society, 1913. Member of the Admiralty's Board of Invention and Research, 1915–18.

16 W. P. Jolly, *Sir Oliver Lodge, Psychical Researcher and Scientist*, London, Constable, 1974, p. 121.

17 E. Whittaker, *The Heaviside Centenary Volume*, London, The Institution of Electrical Engineers, 1950, p . 7.

18 O. J. Lodge, *Past Years*, London, Hodder & Stoughton, 1931, pp. 88 and 211.

19 R. K. de Kosky, 'William Crookes and the fourth state of matter', *Isis*, LXVII, 1976, p. 60.

20 Lodge, *Advancing Science*, p. 111.

21 J. J. O'Neill, *Prodigal Genius: the Life of Nikola Tesla*, London, Neville Spearman, 1968, p. 229.

22 O. J. Lodge, 'Electric radiation from conducting spheres, an electric eye and a suggestion regarding vision', *Nature*, XLI, 1890, pp. 462–3.

23 E. Branly, *Comptes Rendues*, CXI, 1890, pp. 785–7.

24 *The Times*, 8 September 1888.

25 J. C. Maxwell, 'A dynamical theory of the electromagnetic field', *Philos. Trans. R. Soc.*, CLV, 1865, pp. 459–512.

26 O. J. Lodge, 'The ether and its function', *Nature*, XXVII, 1883, pp. 328–30.

27 E. Rutherford, 'A magnetic detector of electric waves, and some of its applications', *The Electrician*, XXXVII, 1896, p. 367.

28 D. Wilson, *Rutherford, Simple Genius*, London, Hodder & Stoughton, 1983, p. 95.

29 G. Marconi, 'Note on a magnetic detector of electric waves which can be employed as a receiver for space telegraphy', *Proc. R. Soc.*, LXX, 1902, pp. 341–2.

30 Jolly, *Sir Oliver Lodge*, pp. 51–2.

31 O'Neill, *Prodigal Genius*, pp. 264–7.

32 E. E. Fournier d'Albe, *Life of Sir William Crookes*, London, Fisher Unwin, 1923, pp. 176–8.

33 Lodge, *Past Years*, pp. 168 and 189.

34 [B. Stewart and P. G. Tait], *The Unseen Universe*, London, Macmillan, 1874.

35 O'Neill, *Prodigal Genius*, p. 260.

36 O. J. Lodge, 'A discussion concerning the motion of the ether near the earth and concerning the connexion between ether and gross matter, with some new experiments', *Phil. Trans. R. Soc.*, CLXXXIV, 1893, pp. 727–804.

37 G. F. Fitzgerald, 'The period of vibration of disturbances of electrification of the earth', *Nature*, XLVIII, 1893, p. 526.

38 J. Erskine-Murray, *A Handbook of Wireless Telegraphy*, London, Crosby Lockwood & Son, 1913, pp. 314–30.

39 Lodge, *Past Years*, p. 337.

40 O'Neill, *Prodigal Genius*, p. 252.

6

Suggestions for the application of scientific discovery

... can be utilised for the transmission of messages

W.H. Preece, 1894

At least one of the Royal Navy's specialist officers realised that contemporary research into the properties of electromagnetic radiation might provide a solution to the service's problems of communicating between vessels. Jackson later reported to his superiors that '... my idea of utilising Hertzian waves for signalling from Torpedo Craft originated in about 1891'.[1] He was prohibited, by national security regulations, from publishing this idea openly in the technical press. In 1892, Jackson left the torpedo school when he was posted to a foreign station, and so was unable to continue his own researches for the time being. But there was also a civil need for a wireless telegraph. This same idea had occured to civilian applied scientists who were free to publish their speculations.

The suggestion of radio telegraphy

On his retirement from the Presidency of the Institution of Electrical Engineers at the beginning of 1892, Crookes published an article[2] summarising his views on the probable future development of electrical engineering. He wrote particularly about the applications of the newly-discovered Hertzian waves. Having advocated scientific research for the solution of social problems during most of his career, he wrote of social as well as technical implications of the developments which he predicted. The article was published in a reformist journal, the *Fortnightly Review*, already well known for its support of such causes as the allocation of public funds for scientific education and research, the expansion of the Royal Navy and the improvement of the coastal rescue services.

As one of the country's leading electrical scientists, it is probable that Crookes was already aware of Trotter's recommendation in *The Electrician*[3] and there are similarities in their choices of words. Where Trotter had remarked that electromagnetic '... radiations would probably pierce not only fog but a brick wall', Crookes commented in his article that '... rays of light will not pierce through a wall, nor, as we know only too well, through a London fog. But the electric vibrations of a yard or more in wavelength ... will easily pierce such mediums ...' But Crookes went further and was more specific than Trotter; the 'flash signals' which Trotter had mentioned were identified more precisely by Crookes as 'messages in the Morse code', and he added that it would be necessary to investigate means of generating waves '... of any desired wavelength from the shortest, say of a few feet in length, which will easily pass through buildings and fogs, to those long waves whose lengths are measured by tens, hundreds and thousands of miles', instead of concentrating studies on the very short, high-frequency waves as used by Hertz and considered by Trotter. According to Crookes, electromagnetic waves could be used not only for emergency signals from light-vessels to the shore but to provide a new system of communications — in Crookes' own words: '... the bewildering possibility of telegraphy without wires, posts, cables, or any of our present costly appliances'. Being an experienced consultant, he recognised the commercial as well as the technical attractions of this proposed new method of signalling.

Crookes's prophetic article discussed the technical feasibility of Hertzian-wave telegraphy, but was published in a popular non-technical journal. Its appearance coincided with the climax of the Royal National Lifeboat Institution's campaign for better coastal communications. 'Before that,' as Aitken says, 'experimentation with electromagnetic waves was essentially a matter of validating Maxwellian theory; after, it became a matter of devising signalling systems, of inventions and patents, of developing a commercial technology.'[4] For Crookes had done more than suggest a new means of telegraphy. He had shown what was needed to implement his suggestions. He said:

What, therefore, remains to be discovered is — firstly, simpler and more certain means of generating electric waves ... secondly, more delicate receivers which will respond to wavelengths between certain defined limits and be silent to all others; thirdly, means of darting the sheaf of rays in any desired direction.

The second of these developments − the 'delicate receivers' − was then explained in more detail:

the correspondents must attune their instruments to a definite wavelength, say, for example, fifty yards. I assume here that the progress of discovery would give instruments capable of adjustment by turning a screw or altering the length of a wire, so as to become receptive of wavelengths of any preconcerted length.

In fact, such a means of tuning already existed. During his 1888 experiments with lightning conductors, Lodge had demonstrated how two adjacent circuits could be tuned to resonance by 'altering the length of a wire'. Despite the cautionary note in the passage cited above, there was little need for further fundamental discovery. As Crookes pointed out:

This is no mere dream of a visionary philosopher. All the requisites needed to bring it within the grasp of daily life are well within the possibilities of discovery, and are so reasonable and so clearly in the path of researches which are now being actively prosecuted in every capital of Europe that we may any day expect to hear that they have emerged from the realms of speculation into those of sober fact.

Tesla and Lodge helped the progress of these ideas into 'sober fact' during the next two years. Crookes had realised that substances opaque to visible light might be transparent to Hertzian radiation of longer wavelength (and consequently of lower frequency). He had deduced that means of generating and receiving radiation of constant wavelength would be needed for reliable communication. But one property of electromagnetic radiation could, it seemed, prevent any such system as Crookes had described from competing effectively with conventional line telegraphs. Rectilinear propagation − the fact that electromagnetic radiation, including light, travels in straight lines − implied that the transmission of information by Hertzian radiation could be limited by the earth's curvature. Telegraphy beyond the optical horizon might still require the 'costly appliances' of 'wires, posts and cables' that Crookes sought to abolish.

One solution to this problem, as it appeared to physicists in the 1890s, would be to increase the wavelength − reduce the frequency − of the electromagnetic waves. Even the earth itself might then be no obstacle to their passage. Fitzgerald had suggested, and Lodge's experiments had been based on the idea, that this result might be attained at a frequency of about $0 \cdot 06$ Hz. This corresponded to a wavelength over 17,000 kilometres, in the range of 'thousands of miles' which Crookes had mentioned. Tesla, who had possibly discussed the problem with Crookes and Lodge, first proposed telegraphy at these extremely low frequencies after returning to the USA from a European lecture tour in 1892. As described to the National Electric Light Association,[5] his suggested wireless system involved the deliberate disturbance of the earth's electrostatic field to produce effects which might be detected at considerable distances from their source. He said that a generator of alternating currents should be connected:

with one of its terminals to earth (conveniently to the water mains), and the other to a body of large surface P. When the electric oscillation is set up there will be a movement of electricity in and out of P, and alternating currents will pass through the earth, converging to, or diverging from, the point C where the ground connection is made. In this manner neighbouring points on the earth's surface will be disturbed. But the disturbance will diminish with the distance, and the distance at which the effect will still be perceptible will depend on the quantity of electricity set in motion. Since the body P is insulated, in order to displace a considerable quantity the potential of the source must be excessive, since there would be limitations as to the surface of P. The conditions might be adjusted so that the generator or source S will set up the same electrical movement as though its circuit were closed. Thus it is certainly practicable to impress an electric vibration of at least a certain low period upon the earth by means of proper machinery ... Now, it is quite certain that at any point within a certain radius of the source S, a properly adjusted self-induction and capacity device can be set in action by resonance.

Tesla was therefore proposing to use a transmitter based on an open-ended oscillating circuit. This would be much as Hertz and Lodge had used, but with a low-frequency alternator instead of an induction coil or a Leyden jar. A tuned receiver would be 'set in action by resonance', as Crookes had suggested. Tesla enlarged on these proposals in a lecture to the Franklin Institute, adding that:

if by means of powerful machinery, rapid variations of the earth's potential were produced, a grounded wire reaching up to some height would be traversed by a current which could be increased by connecting the free end to a body of some size ... The experiment would probably best succeed on a ship at sea. In this manner, even if it were not possible to operate machinery intelligence might be transmitted quite certainly.[6]

The mention of a 'ship at sea' could have been prompted by the ideas for communicating between light-ships and the shore, which had been a subject of interest to Trotter and others during Tesla's visit to Britain. But the hope that it might be possible 'to operate machinery' revealed another line of development. Tesla's invention of the induction motor and other items of alternating-current equipment made possible the use of multiphase power distribution systems. These were being exploited during the late 1880s and early 1890s in large-scale power distribution networks energised from central generating stations (another example of the trend to centralised provision of social services and utilities in the USA as well as in Britain!). Electrical power was reaching small remote communities which could not have benefited from Edison's localised direct-current distribution systems. Low-loss alternating-current transmission and economies of scale meant that these rural customers need pay little more than town-dwellers for their supplies. The system appeared to fulfil the applied scientists' and social reformers' ambition of providing cheap, non-polluting power for every citizen, and Tesla had been responsible for much of its practical development. A wireless power distribution system would reduce expenses further by getting rid, as Crookes suggested, of costly cables and their supports.

But even the dissemination of information over a wide area through such a wireless system would not be possible without more scientific data. Lodge's experiments had failed to detect electromagnetic waves in the earth at the expected frequency of $0 \cdot 06$ Hz. There was some unexpected factor involved. Tesla could not start designing the alternators and receivers needed for his wireless system until he had investigated the conditions for wave propagation within the earth at his Colorado Springs experiments.[7]

A demonstration of radio telegraphy in practice

But there was nothing to prevent the transmission of electromagnetic radiation across shorter ranges. By the end of 1893 both Trotter and Tesla had published proposals for signalling from ships. Trotter was an electric lighting consultant; Tesla had put forward the idea to an audience of electric lighting engineers. Both were aware that Hertzian radiation was the same kind of radiation as visible light. They were no doubt comparing electromagnetic wave transmitters with existing lighthouses and signalling lamps.

Preece used the same analogy when describing the Post Office's wireless telegraphy experiments to the British Association at Oxford on 13 August 1894. As reported in *The Times*, Preece then said that:

The mechanism of the mode of signalling across space is not difficult to follow. Its analogue is a flash of light seen at a distance. Energy is expended, say, in a lighthouse. The energy assumes the luminous form exciting the ether to undulate with a frequency of many millions per second, which acting upon the retina of the eye, produces the sensation called light. The burning of the oil-lamp of the lighthouse is the primary source of energy; the rapid undulations of the ether propagated in straight lines at a velocity of 186,000 miles per second are the radiation, transmitting this energy in a wave form to the distant ship; the eye is the apparatus which transforms the energy of the light waves into a form which excites conciousness in the brain. In our electrical experiments the primary energy is in the current form; the comparatively few alternations per second excite waves in the ether of a few hundreds per second only. But these oscillations of the ether or electric waves are of the same character as those of light; they move with the same velocity, and when they fall on a sympathetic secondary conductor they excite in that conductor currents of electricity of the same frequency: and if a telephone be inserted in that circuit and applied to the ear, sounds and musical notes are distinctly heard which by pre-concerted measures, such as the use of the Morse code, can be utilised for the transmission of messages.[8]

Evidently Preece still believed, as he had in 1892, that his inductive telegraph was producing true Hertzian waves. His disputes with Heaviside and Lodge had not yet been settled – his outburst about the writings of 'visionary mathematicians' in technical journals was made only a few months earlier – and no one, apparently, was willing (or able) to enlighten him.

But the next day, 14 August 1894, members of the Association witnessed the generation and detection of what was undoubtedly Hertzian radiation. A joint meeting of Section A (Physical Sciences) and Section I (Physiology) had been organised to consider the latest theories of light and vision. As reported in *Nature*:

Prof Lodge showed a number of experiments upon the reflection, polarisation and refraction of Hertz waves ... Electromagnetic waves produced by a small vibrator were allowed to fall upon a detector placed inside a large copper 'hat'. The detector consisted of a glass tube containing iron borings forming part of a circuit with a galvanometer. On account of its mode of action, this detector is called by Prof Lodge a 'coherer'. Under the action of the waves, its resistance diminishes and the galvanometer current increases.[9]

The galvanometer mentioned in this account was in fact a Kelvin marine galvanometer, designed as a receiving element in submarine cable telegraphy. It was supplied to Lodge by Alexander Muirhead, manager and scientific adviser in his family's telegraphic instrument business.

Lodge himself described later how this apparatus was demonstrated to his audience:

When the Morse key at the sending end was held down, the rapid trembler of the coil maintained the wave production, and the deflected spot of light at the receiving end remained in its deflected position so long as the key was down; but when the key was only momentarily depressed, a short series of waves was emitted, and the spot of light then suffered a momentary deflection. These long and short signals obviously corresponded to the dashes and dots of the Morse code and thus it was easy to demonstrate the signalling of some letters of the alphabet, so that they could be read by any telegraphist in the audience – some of whom may even now [1931] remember that they did so. [10]

Lodge had shown how Morse signals could be transmitted and received by Hertzian radiation, exactly as Preece had described the day before. Moreover, this demonstration involved a standard Morse key and a Kelvin galvanometer – ordinary telegraphic equipment, though already obsolescent in commercial practice. An audience which included professional scientists and engineers had been given a display of electromagnetic-wave telegraphy which confirmed the practicality of Trotter's and Crookes's proposals.

The delivery of this display was extremely effective. According to the report in *Nature*, 'the audience, which filled every part of the large museum lecture-room, repeatedly showed its appreciation of Prof Lodge's beautiful experiments'. [11] But Lodge himself made no immediate effort to follow up the developments he had demonstrated. He admitted later that he was, at the time, 'satisfied with the knowledge that it could be done', [12] Tesla's laboratory in New York was destroyed by fire on 13 March 1895, and this may have delayed the start of his Colorado Springs investigations. Both were subsequently to experiment with and to patent radio apparatus of their own design, but not until 1897–98. By then Marconi would already have shown the practical value of the techniques which Lodge and Tesla had originated.

The lectures and writings of these applied scientists, however, helped to publicise how much information was available for other experimenters. Hertz died in January 1894, at the early age of thirty-six, but his papers had already been collected together and published in Leipzig.[13] A translation of this book gave a summary of the basic theory and properties of electromagnetic radiation for English-speaking readers.[14] Early in 1894, Lodge provided a further summary of the work and described later studies in an obituary lecture on Hertz delivered at the Royal Institution. This lecture was printed in *The Electrician*[15] and subsequently published separately.[16] These works by Hertz and Lodge provided enough information for anyone to start their own investigations of electromagnetic waves. The books circulated widely, and were cited by Popov in Russia,[17] by Bose in India,[18] and by Jackson in Great Britain.[19]

Psychic research and radio science

Some of Lodge's colleagues believed that it was not enough merely to publicise the details of electromagnetic theory. Lord Rayleigh advised him to continue with his telegraphic experiments, adding that 'there is a life-work in it'.[20] Muirhead, according to his wife's account, could not sleep on the night after the Oxford lecture and 'the next day he went to Lodge with the suggestion that messages could be sent by use of these waves to "feed cables".'[21] But none of these influential people could persuade Lodge to continue the work. His interests were turning from the immediate practical applications to more abstract implications of his studies. As Jolly has observed, during the period 1894–97:

he was more scientist than inventor and when he investigated some phenomenon he hoped to discover that the laws governing it were but a particular example of a wider generality ... he was interested in removing barriers between physics and physiology by showing that parts of the eye might behave analogously to parts of a Hertz receiver. In his work on the ether he looked for a connection between matter and radiation that was later established by relativity theory. Finally, in the widest context, he hoped to show that the ether could in some way be the instrument of uniting the material and spirit worlds.[22]

Lodge's actions in the weeks immediately after the Oxford presentation show that he was then preoccupied with this last interest. He went to France at the invitation of Charles Richet to assist in psychic investigations.

The association between psychic research and radio telegraphy is not discussed at length in existing histories of the technology, and those few studies that do mention the subject refer to it in negative terms. Aitken, for instance, ignores Crookes' interest completely and writes of Lodge that:

It is tempting to speculate as to possible connections between Lodge's early recognition of the importance of resonance in electronics and his well-known later interest in spiritualism, but his writings give scant support for the notion and if there was any connection it was not at the level of consciousness.[23]

But this assessment, with its reference to a 'later' interest, reflects the common misconception that Crookes's and Lodge's interest in spiritualism was a reaction to personal tragedy during the First World War. In fact, they were active psychic researchers in the early 1880s. This was long before the loss of a much-loved wife and son respectively; it was long before Hertz demonstrated the existence of electromagnetic radiation.

Their common interest in psychic research reinforced both the coherence of this small group of applied scientists and their concern with the aether. But it had a more direct influence as well on the development of radio. In 1893, Tesla suggested that telepathy might also be caused by waves similar to Hertzian radiation. Such aether-waves, he argued, produce those impulses in the optic nerve which create visual images on the brain. It is then possible, conversely, that the mental act of visualising an image transmits a signal through the optic nerve to the eye and so creates electromagnetic radiation.[24] Lodge developed this idea, discussing how such a telepathic radiation might be 'received' by another person in words reminiscent of his experiments with resonant circuits:

a vivid impression made upon one person could reverberate and be received by sufficiently sensitive people at a distance; so that, when any tragedy happened to an individual, some information about that tragedy could be conveyed to a relative or to any other interested person who happened to be in a placid or receptive stage.[25]

Crookes, Tesla and Lodge all emphasised the need for similar sensitive, selectively-tuned receivers in their writings on wireless telegraphy. Their realisation of the importance of these devices was reinforced by their psychic researches. Analogies between spirit-messages, telepathy and radio telegraphy are obvious, but these applied scientists believed all three were not only analogous but actual, distinct manifestations of the same physical phenomenon.

The applied scientists' studies of the propagation of electro-magnetic radiation on wires, in free space, and within the earth, were all an attempt to determine the properties of the aether. Lodge's psychic work was part of the same investigation. It was not, in his own view, a diversion from his interest in mathematical physics. Similarly, neither Lodge nor Tesla would have considered their ambitions for recognition as pure physicists to be incompatible with their interests in the application of science to the solution of social problems. But they wanted to resolve some of the outstanding problems of physical theory before considering the practical applications of their work. Transmitting Morse signals over relatively short ranges presented no apparent difficulties. The possibility had been discussed in detail by Trotter in 1891, Crookes in 1892, and Tesla in 1893 before its actual demonstration by Lodge in 1894. There was little theoretical knowledge to be gained, they believed, from the construction of a practical telegraph system. And so this particular development was left to those naval officers and civilian applied scientists who were directly concerned with the urgent need for an improvement in maritime communications.

References

1 Captain H. B. Jackson to Vice-Admiral Sir John Fisher, 28 November 1900 (PRO, ref ADM 116/570).

2 W. Crookes, 'Some possibilities of electricity,' *Fortnightly Review*, LI, 1892, pp. 173–81.

3 A. P. Trotter, *The Electrician*, XXVI, 1891, pp. 685–6.

4 H. G. J. Aitken, *Syntony and Spark – the Origins of Radio*, New York, John Wiley, 1976, p. 114.

5 N. Tesla, 'On light and other high frequency phenomena', *Journal of the Franklin Institute*, CXXXVI, 1893, pp. 1–19, 81–98, 161–77, 259–79, 351–60, 401–12.

6 *Ibid*, p. 267.

7 Charles Süsskind ('The early history of electronics', *IEEE Spectrum*, VI, 1969, p. 71) dismisses Tesla's work with the statement that '... these earlier [laboratory] experiments did not directly affect the development of radio telegraphy: nor did a suggestion made by Nikola Tesla that it might be possible to transmit "intelligible signals or perhaps even power" over large distances without wires if sufficiently high frequencies were employed ...' As explained in Chapter 8, I believe that Tesla's proposals had an important direct influence on Marconi's work, and so I do not agree with Süsskind's assessment on this point.

8 *The Times*, 14 August 1894.

9 Anon, 'Physics at the British Association,' *Nature*, L, 1894, pp. 408 and 463.

10 O. J. Lodge, *Advancing Science*, London, Benn, 1931, p. 164.

11   *Nature*, L, 1894, p. 463.

12   Lodge, *Advancing Science*, p. 123.

13   H. Hertz, *Untersuchungen uber die Ausbreitung der elektrischen Kraft*, Leipzig, Johann Ambrosius Barth, 1892.

14   H. Hertz, *Electric Waves*, London, Macmillan, 1893.

15   O. J. Lodge, 'The work of Hertz and some of his successors,' *The Electrician*, XXXIII, 1894, pp. 153–5, 186–90, 204–5.

16   O. J. Lodge, *The Work of Hertz and His Successors*, London, The Electrician Printing & Publishing Co., 1894.

17   A. S. Popov, *Zh Russ fiz-Khim Obschchestra*, XXVIII, 1896, pp. 1–14.

18   J. C. Bose, 'On the determination of the indices of refraction of various substances for the electric ray,' *Proceedings of the Royal Society*, LIX, 1895, pp. 160–7.

19   'Statement of Captain Jackson's Claims as Regards the Invention of Wireless Telegraphy', appended to a letter from Captain F. T. Hamilton to the C-in-C, Devonport, 28 January 1899 (PRO, ref ADM 116/523).

20   Lodge, *Advancing Science*, p. 122.

21   M. E. Muirhead, *Alexander Muirhead*, Oxford, published privately, 1926, p. 39.

22   W. P. Jolly, *Sir Oliver Lodge, Psychical Researcher and Scientist*, London, Constable, 1974, p. 114.

23   Aitken, *Syntony and Spark*, p. 39.

24   Tesla, *On Light*, pp. 2–4.

25   O. J. Lodge, *Past Years*, London, Hodder & Stoughton, 1931, p. 271.

7

A practical apparatus

a means by which torpedo boats might indicate their approach
                                    HMS *Vernon* Annual Report, 1896

In December 1895 an anonymous editorial article in *The Electrician*
reminded applied scientists that there was still a need for an offshore
wireless telegraph.[1] Again, as in the same columns in 1891, the
author suggested that electromagnetic radiation could be adapted to
satisfy that need. He said that an ingenious technologist might 'devise
a practicable system of electromagnetic light-houses, the receivers on
board ship being some electrical equivalent of the human eye'. The
transmitter could be provided readily by modifying existing laboratory
apparatus. But the receiver would have to be particularly robust for
shipboard use. He recommended that this robust receiver should
incorporate 'the substantial and workmanlike form of "coherer"
designed by Prof Bose' which was described in the same issue of the
journal. This coherer had been designed by Jagadis Chunder Bose
(1858–1937), Professor of Physics at Calcutta University.

Bose's studies of the optical properties of materials at radio
wavelengths were first published in Europe by the Royal Society.[2]
But three later papers in *The Electrician*[3] provided the material for
this suggestion in its editorial columns. The apparatus used a simple
spark-gap transmitter and a coherer which depended on loose contacts
between a series of springs. Bose cited Lodge's book as the source
of his designs. It is not clear why his coherer should be considered
more robust than, for instance, the Branly–Lodge filings tube.
Perhaps the facility for adjusting the contact pressure was thought
to ensure more consistent performance.

The editorial columns of *The Electrician* suggested using Hertzian
waves to solve the merchant fleet's offshore signalling problems. Yet
these articles may actually have contributed more to the development
of communications in the Royal Navy than for merchant shipping.

Soon after the appearance of the 1895 feature, and some eight years after the Livathi Bay trials which first revealed the difficulties of signalling between torpedo boats, Henry Jackson started to investigate possible wireless telegraph systems for the Fleet. Five years later, he told Admiral Fisher that:

my idea of utilising Hertzian waves for signalling from Torpedo Craft originated in about 1891, and I should have started experimenting in this direction earlier than I did (in 1895),[4] had I had the time and instruments at my disposal and had I heard of the Coherer principle sooner, the first time I heard of it being through reading some of Dr Bose's experiments in 1895. This important detail was all that was required, in my mind, to obtain signals by Hertzian waves from a distant vessel under way.[5]

The coincidence of dates suggests that his interest, both in 1891 and in 1895, was aroused by reading the articles in *The Electrician*. This supposition is strengthened by the reference to Bose's coherer. Jackson was also to use glass or pitch lenses in his early transmitters, making an apparatus similar to the suggested 'lighthouses'.

Sources of scientific information

Jackson, as a naval officer, had received a sound scientific training. He had made better use of his educational opportunities than had many of his colleagues. Too many officers of the Royal Navy then relied on social rather than technical skills for their advancement. But Jackson's background meant that he was nevertheless as much an 'outsider' within the electrical profession as were Crookes, Heaviside and Lodge. His technical education started in 1868, at the age of thirteen, when he entered HMS *Britannia*. A brief spell on active service during the Zulu War of 1878–79 was followed by a posting to the torpedo school, HMS *Vernon*. Completing the electrical course in 1883, Jackson was appointed to the staff of HMS *Vernon* and admitted to the Institution of Electrical Engineers. Unlike his contemporaries in the Post Office and the Army he was not qualified for better than Associate membership. Indeed, he was not advanced to full membership until 1902, the year after his election to Fellowship of the Royal Society. A naval technical training did not then confer the same professional status as a Post Office apprenticeship.

But Jackson's social standing, both in the Royal Navy and among the community in general, was impeccable. His family of Yorkshire farmers were sufficiently well-to-do[6] and well-connected to secure the personal introduction needed to sit the entrance examination for HMS *Britannia*. Later, he gained some useful scientific contacts. He had made the acquaintance of John Tyndall's friend, T.A. Hirst, who was then a lecturer at the Royal Naval College, Greenwich. In 1890 he married Alice Burbury, the daughter of a Cambridge-educated mathematician.

Jackson's father-in-law, Samuel Burbury (1831–1911) was called to the Bar after graduation, but continued his mathematical studies. He corresponded with several of his Cambridge contemporaries, particularly with Henry Watson (1827–1903), who had qualified as a mathematician before entering the church. Burbury and Watson published a substantial *Mathematical Theory of Electricity and Magnetism* at Oxford in 1889. Jackson's aquaintance with the family had therefore started at about the time when Burbury was absorbed in the study of Maxwell's theory (which formed the basis of his own book) and Jackson was a newly-qualified electrical engineer, no doubt enthusiastically interested in any information that related to his own studies. It was about this time, in 1890, that Burbury was elected a Fellow of the Royal Society. He was a useful source of instruction, a means of access to scientific publications, and possibly a contact with the country's leading scientists, at the period when Jackson has recorded that he first became aware of the potential uses of Hertzian radiation. These family connections could have provided him with information to start his own researches, even if he were not a reader of *The Electrician*. Having begun the work, Jackson then, by his own account, 'extracted much useful information from Professor Lodge's work on Hertz's experiments, and from Hertz's book on oscillations, but certainly no idea of Morse signals being possible'.[7]

The early experiments at Devonport

Whether he learned of Bose's work from the pages of *The Electrician* or, with his father-in-law's aid, from the publications of the Royal Society, Jackson would have had little opportunity for radio research during 1892–94, when he was serving at sea on a foreign station. He returned to Britain early in 1895, when he took command of the torpedo training ship HMS *Defiance* at Devonport. Here he had better facilities for experimenting than were available to an officer in a seagoing warship. There was soon more to show for his efforts than he had achieved in the previous five years. Starting serious research in December 1895, with what he described as 'a coherer of springs' and 'a toy induction coil giving a 1-inch spark' (evidently replicas of Bose's apparatus) he admitted that at first his results were 'not very encouraging'. But he persevered, and by March 1896 had acquired a more powerful induction coil, a re-made coherer and 'lenses constructed of glass or pitch, for the purpose of concentrating the rays'.[8] These improved the performance of his equipment considerably.

By the summer, he was using a completely new receiver. Its coherer was a 'glass tube with a reduced quantity of tin and iron filings mixed', and 'at the same time' Jackson 'adopted a sensitive electric trembling bell to de-cohere the coherer, having previously tapped with his finger to effect that purpose'. He also abandoned the pitch lenses, as 'quite by accident ... he discovered a great advantage was gained by collecting the rays on long conductors not in the circuit, he having, for convenience of handling, connected long stiff copper wires to the terminals of the coherer, sliding the connecting wires along them'.[9] In modern terminology, he had discovered by observation and deduction what would now be called a radio aerial. Other experimenters (such as Popov in Russia and Marconi in Italy) made the same discovery at about the same time. But Jackson's work was quite independent. His experience had a major influence on the design of aerials for Marconi's commercial radio systems about a year later. The filings coherer and its associated decohering electric bell could, however, have been derived from Lodge's suggestion in 1894 that 'by mounting an electric bell or other vibrator on the same board as a tube of filings, it is possible to arrange so that a feeble electric stimulus shall produce a feeble steady effect, a stronger stimulus a stronger effect, and so on'.[10] Jackson first successfully transmitted and received Morse signals on 20 August 1896.[11] Though the range was quite small (across the after-cabin of HMS *Defiance*, according to the recollections of his colleagues), it was enough to confirm the practicability of this method of signalling. By the end of the month, having improved the apparatus in detail, he was sending intelligible signals over the whole length of HMS *Defiance*. A report from Jackson to the Commander-in-Chief, Devonport,[12] mentions that lenses were used as well as aerials in these later trials; the maximum recorded range was just under fifty metres.

A formal report (with high security classification) of Jackson's experiments circulated among the Royal Navy's torpedo officers in the autumn of 1896. It stated that:

a series of interesting experiments have been carried out by 'Defiance' to ascertain if it were feasible to transmit electric radiations to a distance without any conducting wires, the object being to provide a means by which torpedo boats might indicate their approach or proximity to friendly ships. The 'Defiance' had constructed apparatus by which Morse signals could be slowly transmitted and recorded at short distances; and subsequently trials of apparatus by Signor Marconi, an Italian gentleman, were attended.[13]

Jackson first met Marconi at a War Office conference on 31 August 1896,[14] soon after the successful transmissions in HMS *Defiance*. He then discovered that the young 'Italian gentleman' had been working at Hertzian-wave telegraphy since 1894. Marconi's apparatus was of similar design but superior performance to the *Defiance* system. But Marconi found the information which Jackson had derived from his own experiments both interesting and useful. The two inventors thereafter co-operated closely in their researches. Independent development of the Devonport system may conveniently be considered to have come to an end.

These experiments on board HMS *Defiance* attracted the favourable attention of Jackson's superiors. He was already regarded as one of the more promising of the younger generation of officers. Promoted to Captain in 1896, at the relatively early age of forty-one, he was evidently expected to attain flag rank and lead part of Fisher's expanded fleet. The successful Devonport trials had shown him to be an experimental applied scientist of high standard. He was exactly the sort of officer needed, it was thought, to command the squadrons of a technologically-based navy.

Later proclaimed by Fisher to be one of the 'seven best brains in the Navy',[15] Jackson was already, in the 1890s, in a position to influence the Royal Navy's technical policies. In the early twentieth century, he was entrusted with a leading role implementing the most far-reaching programme of naval reforms since the transition from sail to steam.

Popov's radio experiments for the Russian Navy

This study is concerned with the British radio industry. But it is interesting to compare Jackson's researches with similar work at the same period by Popov for the Russian Navy. The Imperial Russian fleet was then the third largest in the world. Its equipment was much the same as that of the Royal Navy (indeed, many of its ships had been built or fitted-out in British yards). Russian strategy, however, was very different. The navy's main task was to defend a long coast-line rather than to defend merchant ships. Russia's few ocean-going battleships were not intended to engage in fleet actions at sea. Reinforced by some twenty coastal defence vessels, they would operate only at short distances from their harbours. As the Royal Navy had discovered in 1888, the inland telegraphs could then be used to co-ordinate their operations. Torpedo boats were not believed to be a threat to this battlefleet − a belief soon to be confounded by the Japanese flotillas at Port Arthur − but the means of offsetting its numerical inferiority. During their researches, Jackson and Popov used many of the same sources of information and worked in similar circumstances. But Popov was less concerned with useful results. His career as a lecturer and an experimenter was more comparable with that of Lodge.

Alesandr Popov (1859−1906) came from much the same middle-class background as Lodge, but had received a more formal scientific education. The son of a priest, he graduated in mathematics at the University of St Petersburgh (now Leningrad) followed, in 1882, with further study in the post-graduate school of physics. Being, however, unable to concentrate on the electrical research which was already his chief interest, he left after a year to take a lecturer's post at the Imperial Navy's torpedo school in Kronstadt. Eventually, in 1900, he returned to St Petersburg as Professor of Physics. After seventeen years of productive work teaching naval engineers, it seems that Popov (like so many of his contemporaries in Britain and the USA) still cherished the ambition of achieving distinction as a pure physicist.

Soon after publication of Hertz's papers in 1887−88, Popov constructed a replica of Hertz's apparatus. He used it in his lectures to demonstrate the properties of electro-magnetic waves. In 1890 he was asked to repeat these lectures to an audience of naval officers in St Petersburg. According to an account published in Moscow some fifty years later, the content of this talk included 'Conditions for resonant discharge. Induction at the resonant discharge − electrical resonance phenomenon. Wire transmission of electrical oscillations. Propagation of electric oscillations through a non-conducting medium − electric rays. Polarization, reflection and refraction of electric rays.'[16] Popov's presentation therefore covered the properties of radiation both on guiding wires and in free space. It showed that he was aware of the work of Lodge as well as that of Hertz.

Popov could have learned of Lodge's research from English-language technical journals. Foreign entrepreneurs and craftsmen were encouraged to establish businesses in Russia and train their employees in the techniques of modern industry. As in Britain, ship-building made a major contribution to the development of applied science. Despite the naval rivalry between the two countries, British firms were responsible (directly or through their local subsidiaries) for the expansion of the Russian fleet in the late nineteenth century. This industrial growth was supported by an increase in the facilities for technical education; there were only eight technical colleges in the whole of Russia in 1894, but the number increased to more than a hundred over the following ten years.[17] Much of the information needed in these colleges was imported, some of it from Britain.

Popov cited an article by Lodge from *The Electrician* in one of his own papers in 1896,[18] published a letter in the same journal in 1897,[19] and may have read a letter from Elihu Thomson, the well-known American engineer, which also was printed in *The Electrician* in July 1894. Describing problems experienced at an electro-plating works during a thunderstorm, Thomson pointed out that poor contacts in the plating baths would act like a coherer. 'The incident', he added, 'suggests the use of Dr Lodge's ingenious instrument in the study of the waves which are propagated during thunder-storms.'[20] Popov constructed such an apparatus in the spring of 1895. This wave-detector was installed at the Meteorological Obser-vatory of the Forestry Institute at St Petersburg in July 1895, Popov having already written a brief note of the coherer circuits it used.[21] He provided a more complete account in the following January. This described how the lightning conductor at the Institute

by means of a wire carried first on the wood of the mast, and further stretched across the yard on insulators into the meteorological observatory, was connected with the apparatus [while the opposite terminal of the coherer] was connected to a wire which served as an earth conductor or connection for the other meteorological apparatus, and was connected to the water supply pipes.[22]

The circuit of this detector was published in *The Electrician* about two years later.

Thus Popov had designed a circuit very similar to the radio receiver which Jackson was to derive independently a year later in 1896.

It used an aerial, as would the Devonport system, but it also included an associated earth connection. Popov's paper of January 1896 acknowledged that the coherer and its de-cohering electric bell were based on Lodge's proposals; his circuit, however, made more positive provision for de-coherence than Lodge's reliance on tremors conveyed through the common baseboard.

This lightning detector was, in effect, an untuned radio receiver. Indeed, at the end of his 1896 paper, Popov himself remarked that '... I can express my hope that my apparatus will be applied for signalling on great distances by electric vibrations as soon as there will be invented a more powerful generator of such vibrations'. This hope was to be realised, and perhaps sooner than Popov had expected.

His signalling range, however, could not be described as a 'great distance'. On 24 March 1896, Popov described his researches to the Russian Physical–Chemical Society. He showed them the lightning detector, connecting its output to a Morse instrument which provided a permanent record of its signals. A spark transmitter was used as a source of Hertzian radiation to show the apparatus in operation. Some of the audience later recalled that Popov manipulated his transmitter to generate Morse symbols for the words 'Heinrich Hertz'.[23] Nearly six months before Jackson's first successful transmission, radio signalling had been demonstrated to a Russian audience.

The circumstances of this demonstration were similar to those of Lodge's presentation at Oxford in 1894. Popov's behaviour after the lecture was also reminiscent of Lodge's actions. He seems to have made no immediate attempt to improve his apparatus for telegraphic use. Instead, he spent his summer vacation as usual, superintending the power plant for the annual fair at Nizhni Novgorod. There is no record of any further electromagnetic wave research by Popov before the autumn of 1896.[24] He was evidently not then under any pressure from his employers, the Russian Navy, to produce a practical signalling system. The strategic plans of a fleet organised primarily for coastal defence did not depend on improved communications. Moreover, Popov, like Lodge, was more interested at the time in the implications of his studies for pure physics. Lodge and Popov had shown that existing laboratory apparatus was able to transmit and receive Morse signals. But they both still needed some catalyst to promote the combination of their scientific knowledge with the existing social needs in order to produce a useful wireless telegraph system.

References

1 Anon, *The Electrician*, XXXVI, 1895, p. 273.

2 J. C. Bose, 'On the determination of the indices of refraction of various substances for the electric ray', *Proc. Roy. Soc.*, LIX, 1895, pp. 160–7.

3 J. C. Bose, 'On polarisation of electric rays by double refracting crystals'; 'On double refraction of the electric ray by a strained dielectric'; 'On a new electro-polariscope', *The Electrician*, XXXVI, 1895, pp. 289–90, 290–1, 291–2.

4 The bracketed phrase '... (in 1895)...' is in the original, and not a later interpolation.

5 H. B. Jackson to Vice-Admiral Sir John Fisher, 28 November 1900 (PRO ref. ADM 116/570).

6 A. J. Marder, *From the Dreadnought to Scapa Flow*, Oxford, Oxford University Press, 1961, pp. 30–1.

7 'Statement of Captain Jackson's Claims as Regards the Invention of Wireless Telegraphy', appended to a letter from Captain F. T. Hamilton to the C-in-C Devonport, 28 January 1899 (PRO, ref. ADM 116/523).

8 *Ibid.*

9 *Ibid.*

10 O. J. Lodge, *The Work of Hertz and His Successors,* London, The Electrician Printing & Publishing Co., 1894, p. 27.

11 'Tabular Statement of Dates of Working Out Important Points of *'Defiance'*'s' System', (PRO, ref. ADM 116/523).

12 Captain H. B. Jackson to C-in-C Devonport, 16 September 1896 (PRO, ref. ADM 116/523).

13 'Annual Report of the Torpedo School (HMS *Vernon*)' for 1896, p. 71 (NHL).

14 H. B. Jackson to C-in-C Devonport, 16 September 1896 (PRO, ref. ADM 116/523).

15 The other 'best brains' were those of four naval officers – Jellicoe, Bacon, Maddern and Henderson – and two civilians – Gard and Gracie. These seven were appointed by Fisher, when he became First Sea Lord, to a committee considering the design of ships required in future naval conflicts – the committee which introduced Dreadnought battleships and submarines (among other new types) into the Royal Navy. All five officers eventually reached the rank of Admiral of the Fleet.

16 *Collected Documents relating to the Invention of Radio by A. S. Popov*, Moscow, 1945, p. 47, cited by B. Vvedensky, 'A. S. Popov', *The Great Soviet Encyclopaedia* (English translation), 1955.

17 C. Trebilcock, *The Industrialization of the Continental Powers*, London, Longman, 1981, pp. 282–3.

18 C. Süsskind, 'Popov and the beginnings of radiotelegraphy', *Proceedings of the Institute of Radio Engineers*, 1962, pp. 2039–40.

19 A. S. Popoff (sic) 'An application of the coherer', *The Electrician*, XL, 1897, p. 235.

20 E. Thomson, 'Hertzian waves in laboratories and electro-plating works', *The Electrician*, XXXIII, 1894, 304–5.

21 Süsskind, *Popov*, p. 2039.
22 English translation in J. A. Fleming, *Principles of Electric Wave Telgraphy*, London, Longmans, 1906, p. 425.
23 V. S. Gabel, *Wireless World*, XVIII, 1926, p. 319.
24 Süsskind, *Popov*, p. 2040.

8

The principal catalyst

a young Italian of the name of Marconi
A. Campbell Swinton, 1896

There was a marked revival of interest in radio telegraphy during 1897. Tesla, Popov and Lodge resumed their experiments, while Jackson made extensive modifications to the design of his system. Publicity for the work of a young Italian inventor, Guglielmo Marconi (1874–1937), caused this renewal of effort. Marconi's success was the principal catalyst promoting the combination of separate elements into a commercial industry.

He came from the same sort of middle-class background as many British applied scientists of the later nineteenth century. His father was an Italian landowner and his mother came from the Jameson family of Irish whiskey distillers. Marconi's upbringing reflected the difference between his parents' backgrounds; he was baptised a Catholic at his father's insistence but educated as a Protestant in accordance with his mother's wishes. Much of his radio research was carried out at his family home, the Villa Grifone near Bologna. As he had no paid employment during this period (1894–96), the research was, in effect, financed by his family. There seems to have been some friction between Marconi and his father, but nothing more than can be explained by a parent's natural anxiety for a twenty-year-old son to become self-supporting.

Like several of his British contemporaries, Marconi did not receive a full-time university education. Having failed the university entrance examinations, his only formal scientific training was at the Technical Lyceum at Livorno (Leghorn). Nevertheless, he aspired to achieve recognition as a scientist rather than as a practical engineer. His biographers later wrote of him that 'He looks on science as one of the means of explaining some of the wonders which God has allowed in the world, and he believes that when the human brain is endowed with the ability to make great scientific discoveries, it is the will and direction of God.'[1] Marconi was a public figure (and saying what he thought was expected of him) when this statement was published. Nevertheless, it appears that Marconi regarded pure science, in the conventional way, as an aspect of natural theology. His ambitions, like his family and his education, were not very dissimilar from those of Crookes, Lodge and Tesla. And, like them, he was an advocate of radical social reform. Eventually, indeed, he became a prominent member of his country's Fascist party.

Marconi's biographers also record that his early ambition was to be a naval officer. He was disappointed, as he had been in his hopes of a university education, when he was rejected by the Italian naval authorities, but he retained a keen interest in maritime affairs all his life. He received his technical education at Livorno, adjacent to the naval base at La Spezia. His hobbies – sea-fishing and yachting – were those of a sailor. Several of his close friends, including Jackson in Britain and Luigi Solari (1875–1957) in Italy, were naval officers. He would have found ample opportunity, as a young man, for indulging his interests. Italy, the naval ally of Britain, was itself experiencing a cultural 'maritime myth' associated with an expansion of shipbuilding. British investment in Italian industry and State subsidies produced a nine-fold increase in the annual output of Italian shipyards between 1896 and the end of the nineteenth century.[2] The large engineering works built by Armstrong for the naval dockyard at Pozzuoli in 1885 was followed by similar support from British armaments companies for the yards at Ansaldo and La Spezia. English-language periodicals circulated among Italian technical colleges and libraries, in addition to all the financial aid for Italian industry. Marconi, through his mother's influence, was fluent in English. He could read these journals avidly.

Experiments in Italy

Yet Marconi first learned of the work of Hertz from an Italian-language account. He was only twenty years old at the time. Some forty years later, he recalled that

the idea of transmitting messages through space by means of electric waves came to me suddenly as a result of having read in an Italian electrical journal about the work and experiments of Hertz ... It was a long and interesting article; Hertz had just died – actually in the preceding January. The idea obsessed me more and more ... I did not attempt any experiments until we returned to the Villa Grifone in the autumn, but then two large rooms at the top of the house were set aside for me by my mother. And there I began experiments in earnest.[3]

The statement that 'Hertz had just died' suggests that the article was published fairly early in 1894. A contribution which corresponds with Marconi's recollection was printed in the journal *Il Nuovo Cimento* at this time. To be more exact, there were two consecutive contributions; an obituary of Hertz and a description of experiments illustrating Hertz's discoveries.[4] The second of these two articles gave fairly detailed specifications for the construction of simple receivers and transmitters. Augusto Righi (1850–1920), its author, did not suggest using a coherer as receiver, preferring a Geissler tube. Presumably the coherer was not popularised until *after* Lodge's lectures that summer. Indeed, Righi did not cite a single British publication, which is consistent with Marconi's sharp assertion (in a private conversation with Jackson) that he had not heard of Lodge '... in Italy, where possibly Dr Lodge's work and name were less well known than he thinks possible'.[5] His influence is evident, nevertheless, in the transmitter, with a four-ball spark-gap very similar to Lodge's design of 1890. Righi modified this spark-gap slightly, adding an insulating oil-bath between the two centre balls. Marconi used virtually the same insulated spark-gap for his own transmitter.

Marconi did not, however, use a Geissler tube in his receiver. He soon learned of the coherer and, by his own account 'tried about 500 different substances before obtaining ... satisfactory results'.[6] This was a good example of his capacity, which Lodge later identified, for working 'enthusiastically and persistently'.[7] He eventually decided on a glass tube about 38 mm long and of 3 mm internal diameter, containing a mixture of nickel and silver filings. As explained in the subsequent patent specification, this equipment was de-cohered after each received signal 'automatically employing the current which the sensitive tube ... had allowed to begin to flow under the influence of the electric oscillations from the transmitting instrument to work a trembler (similar to that of an electric bell) which hits the tube and so stops the current'.[8] Marconi had therefore arrived at the same circuit arrangements as developed separately by Popov and Jackson. It seems probable that all three were derived from Lodge's book, although Marconi's source may not have acknowledged its debt.

By the summer of 1895, having reproduced some of Hertz's results in his attic laboratories at the Villa Grifone, Marconi started more ambitious experiments in its grounds. He had access to the library in the nearby University of Bologna, and may have attended lectures there by Righi, the Professor of Physics. His studies in the library suggested modifications to his apparatus. Righi had suggested mounting transmitter and receiver at the foci of parabolic reflectors. Marconi found that he achieved greater ranges when '... he connected one terminal of the secondary circuit of his induction coil to a metal plate or net laid on the ground, and the other by a wire to a metal can or cylinder placed on the summit of a pole'.[9] According to his friend, Solari, this arrangement was intended to generate longer wavelengths at the transmitter. The receiver was similarly connected between an elevated conductor and earth to increase its sensitivity to these longer waves. With these modifications, the performance of this system was better than that of any other experimenter at the time. Marconi noted that 'in 1895, I was using an oscillator having one pole earthed and the other connected to an insulated capacity, the receiver also earthed and connected to a similar capacity ... reliable signals could be obtained at 2,400 metres all round, equal to about a mile and a half.[10] In short, Marconi had, like Popov and Jackson, added aerials to his apparatus. He described its operation as:

When transmitting through the air, and it is desired that the signal or electrical action should only be sent in one direction ... I place the oscillation producer at the focus or focal line of a reflector directed to the receiving station ... When transmitting through the earth or water I connect one end of the oscillation producer and one end of the tube or contact [ie, the coherer] to earth and the other ends to conductors or plates, preferably similar to each other, in the air and insulated from earth.[11]

Four significant lines of reasoning are evident in Marconi's description of his work during the summer of 1895. There was, firstly, an attempt to increase the working wavelength. Secondly, there was the reiterated insistence on the same, or similar, capacitance at transmitter and receiver (needed to 'tune' both to operate at the same wavelength). In the third place, there was the addition of elevated metal plates and earth connections to transmitter and receiver. Finally, Marconi believed that with this circuit arrangement the signals were transmitted through the earth or water. All four concepts had been vital parts of Tesla's suggested system of wireless telegraphy in 1893. Although he never discussed the origins of these ideas, Marconi may well have been familiar with Tesla's proposals.

By the end of 1895, Marconi had thus constructed a wireless telegraph which worked with reasonable reliability over useful ranges. But the Ministry of Posts and Telegraphs in Rome were not interested in the apparatus.

Marconi's cousin, Henry Jameson-Davis, later recalled that 'I was in considerable practice as an engineer in London and his mother wrote asking if I could help him; I replied that I would be glad to do what I could if he came to London to see me.'[12] Accordingly, Marconi decided to be a temporary emigrant. Accompanied by his mother, he travelled from Italy to Britain in February 1896.

Approaches to the British Government

Marconi may have known that the British Post Office were seeking a system of maritime communications. He could read British journals (such as *The Times* and *The Electrician*) which publicised the coastal telegraphy problem and described Preece's experiments. Even if he were not familiar with the British technical press, he may have seen the problem mentioned in Italian-language periodicals. It is therefore possible that Marconi arrived in Britain with the intention of approaching the British postal authorities.

But, even if he had not formulated any such definite plan, there was nothing very unusual about a young Italian removing abroad. One-and-a-half million Italians left their native country during the 1890s, by far the largest rate of emigration from any European nation. Indeed, Trebilcock suggests that this movement of personnel was an important factor in the late nineteenth-century expansion of the Italian economy. He says that 'the transfer of Italians to higher-earning occupations overseas achieved this unusual effect by encouraging the repatriation of "foreign" income to relatives still in the homeland'.[13] Marconi's eventual employment as a director and principal shareholder in a British engineering company may be considered as just an extreme example of this practice. In any case, Marconi (like other Italian young men) was then liable for compulsory military service. A trip abroad would postpone this unwelcome prospect and enable him to consult his mother's family about the commercial exploitation of his invention.

Geddes[14] suggests that Marconi was already contemplating his wireless system as being something more than a method of offshore telegraphy when he left Italy. This implies that Marconi was conscious of the lucrative potential market offered by Britain's large navy and merchant fleet. There is, however, no direct evidence that this was in fact Marconi's intention as early as February 1896, and there is little to support the idea in his subsequent activities. He would not then have known of the Royal Navy's need for a wireless telegraph (which was mentioned only in documents with high security classification), and he had not necessarily considered the idea of wireless communication between merchant ships at sea. Neither topic had been discussed widely in the press. There is no record of any approach from Marconi to a merchant shipping line until the spring of 1897.

Instead, he sought the assistance of A.A. Campbell Swinton, a prominent consulting engineer, probably at the suggestion of Jameson-Davies. Recognising that Marconi's system might provide a solution to the coastal communication problem, Campbell Swinton gave him a letter of introduction to Preece:

I am taking the liberty of sending to you with this note a young Italian of the name of Marconi, who has come over to this country with the idea of getting taken up a new system of telegraphy without wires, at which he has been working. It appears to be based on the use of Hertzian waves, and Oliver Lodge's coherer, but from what he tells me, he appears to have got considerably beyond what I believe other people have done in this line.

It has occurred to me that you might possibly be kind enough to see him and hear what he has to say, and I also think that what he has done will very likely be of interest to you.[15]

There are several interesting details in this letter. To begin with, there is the date – 30 March. Marconi described (and may have demonstrated) his apparatus to Campbell Swinton within a few days of Popov's lecture-room demonstration of Morse signalling on 24 March 1896. Neither established any significant priority of disclosure to a third party. Further, it is obvious from the references to Hertzian waves and Oliver Lodge's coherer that Campbell Swinton understood enough electromagnetic theory to appreciate how such a system worked, even if Preece were not so well-informed. It might also be deduced from the letter that Marconi was willing, at this stage in his work, to transfer any rights in the use of his apparatus to the Post Office (rather as the Bretts had sought to sell the rights in their telegraph system to the British government). He seems to have had no objection to telling Campbell Swinton important details of its construction. However, he had already filed a provisional patent specification to secure some protection for his own interests.[16]

Having acquired this letter of introduction, Marconi then also advised the army of his invention. This may have been suggested by Campbell Swinton, who was in contact with the army's electrical engineers and had lectured to them about Tesla's researches.[17] Marconi wrote to the War Office in May 1896, offering what he described as 'electrical devices which enable me to guide or steer a self propelled boat or torpedo from the shore or from a vessel without any person being on the said boat or torpedo'.[18] All coastal defences were then the responsibility of the army. They might therefore be expected to show an interest in this early example of a radio-guided missile controlled 'from the shore'. But the officer appointed to investigate Marconi's offer, Major C. Penrose, then Assistant Inspector of Submarine Defences, was more impressed by the demonstration of his wireless telegraph.[19] Accordingly, a meeting to consider military uses of this system was arranged by the War Office's Torpedo Committee for 31 August 1896. At this meeting, Penrose introduced Marconi to Major G.A. Carr, Instructor in Electricity from the School of Military Engineering at Chatham, and to Jackson, who attended as the Royal Navy's representative. Jackson later reported that 'on seeing Mr Marconi's apparatus ... [he] found that they were practically at the same point, the former being slightly more advanced in details'.[20]

Thus by the late summer of 1896 Marconi was in contact with several influential engineers: Preece from the General Post Office, Penrose from the Royal Engineers and Jackson from the Royal Navy. He could reasonably hope to find a customer for his wireless telegraph from at least one of these government departments.

British reactions to Marconi's work

Marconi had been in Britain for six months, but his methods were known only by a few people. In fact, the very existence of his wireless telegraph system was not generally known until 22 September 1896. Preece then told the British Association at Liverpool that

> ... a young Italian, Signor Marconi, described to him experiments in which he had, by means of Hertzian waves, transmitted signals to a great distance ... he had succeeded in producing electric waves and reflecting them from one parabolic mirror to another one-and-a-quarter mile [2 kilometres] distant. At the latter place they fell on a receiving apparatus which actuated a relay and produced Morse signals.[21]

It was not to be expected that this statement would pass without remark. At the end of the following day's formal session, Lodge, no doubt remembering his own display of Morse signalling to the British Association in August 1894, commented that there was little original in the details of Marconi's methods. He invited those present to attend a demonstration at which he had arranged laboratory apparatus to give similar results. This demonstration helped to exacerbate the ill-feeling which still existed between Lodge and Preece, for when Kelvin accepted Lodge's invitation this scientific 'lion' was in consequence obliged to excuse himself from attending a presentation by Preece![22] Evidently, memories of the lightning-conductor controversy in the 1880s still rankled. A few months later, Lodge repeated his accusation that Marconi's work was not entirely original. But this time his sarcasm was more marked and more clearly directed at Preece. Writing what was ostensibly an historical survey of some technical aspects of radio telegraphy, Lodge claimed that by 1894 contemporary physics research had left only a few practical details of a telegraph system to be settled. 'These details', Lodge suggested, 'could safely be left to those who had charge of the Government monopoly of telegraphs, especially as their eminent Head was known to be interested in this kind of subject.' However, he went on, Preece was '... too busy to remember what had recently been done in the Hertz-wave direction' and so had presented Marconi's work to the British Association under the impression that it were something entirely novel.[23]

Lodge later acknowledged Marconi's achievement by admitting that while he had himself had 'been satisfied with the knowledge that it could be done, Mr Marconi went on enthusiastically and persistently till he made it a practical success'.[24] His bitterest comments were reserved for Preece. Other telegraph engineers and physicists were more ready to criticise the claims of the Italian inventor, especially after the publication of his full patent specification in the summer of 1897. An editorial article in *The Electrician* left no doubt that its author believed there to be nothing original in the patent:

It is reputed to be easy enough for a clever lawyer to drive a coach and four through an Act of Parliament. If this patent be upheld in the courts of law it will be seen that it is equally easy for an eminent patent-counsel to compile a valid patent from the publicly described and exhibited products of another man's brain.[25]

Others followed the lead given by this article. J. J. Thomson reminded readers of the *Daily Chronicle* that his own pupil, Rutherford, had transmitted and detected Hertzian waves over substantial ranges before anyone (in Britain) had heard of Marconi.[26] Minchin claimed[27] in *The Electrician* that he had himself discovered the principle of the radio aerial as early as 1891 − a claim supported by Appleyard.[28] Benest, also interested in the origins of the radio aerial, described the use of elevated conductors for wireless telegraphy by Edison in 1892.[29] Even Campbell Swinton would not allow Marconi's patent to go entirely unchallenged, commenting[30] that Tesla, too, had suggested using aerial capacitances insulated from the earth's surface.

Only one correspondent, Captain J. N. Kennedy of the Royal Engineers, wrote in support of Marconi during this discussion in the pages of *The Electrician*. Kennedy pointed out that Marconi had demonstrated in practice the advantages of elevated aerial wires at both transmitter and receiver. Minchin's experiments had, he said, involved horizontal wires at the receiver alone.[31] Throughout the summer of 1897, as Jackson later reminded Marconi, '... everyone seemed against the system, except you, I and Capt Kennedy'.[32] The popular press were then taking an interest in Marconi's work. Practical electricians seemed, however, no more willing to accept Marconi's claims than to accept the electromagnetic theories of his precursors.

The controversy which started in 1897 has continued, in modified form, to the present day. Several historians have disputed the claim that Marconi was the 'inventor of radio'. Russian authors, with the support at times of the Soviet government, prefer the name of Popov. Others, notably in Yugoslavia and the USA, suggest instead that Tesla should be accorded this title. At least one British writer has claimed that Jackson was the true inventor.[33] The nationalistic aspects of these proposals are obvious, but each is also based on at least some evidence of priority. Marconi filed his fundamental patent in June 1896. Tesla had described his suggested system in lectures and in print (and subsequently designed *some* of its components) about three years before that date; Jackson had started experiments and reported the fact to his superiors seven months earlier; Popov described and operated his lightning detector a year earlier, and had used it as a radio receiver in a demonstration three months before Marconi filed his patent. But, unintentionally, these various claims also help to establish Marconi's status within the world-wide radio industry. His work was a standard against which others' achievements might be measured.

Indeed the publicity given to his work was sometimes a contribution towards these other innovators' achievements.

The revival of radio research

Lodge re-started his interrupted radio researches late in 1896. The news of Marconi's progress was a more effective incentive than either Rayleigh's or Muirhead's exhortations had been two years previously. He patented his own system of Hertzian-wave telegraphy in the spring of 1897.[34] Popov, too, learned of Marconi's work in the autumn of 1896 — so far as is known, by reading a report in a Russian newspaper while working at the Nizhni Novgorod fair. According to one of his colleagues,[35] he was startled by the news. He took up his own studies once more on returning to Kronstadt, and soon wrote to a local newspaper, pointing out that his lightning detector was probably very similar to Marconi's receiver. His experiments were evidently carried out with the knowledge and approval of his superiors. In the spring of 1897 he was allowed to conduct trials of his apparatus in Kronstadt harbour on board ships of the Russian Navy.

The temporary hiatus in Lodge's and Popov's work thus ended in the autumn of 1896 — at about the same time as Jackson was introduced to Marconi at the War Office meeting. Tesla, too, resumed work early in 1897. His investigations were mentioned in an American technical journal during that summer.[36] The wording of the article suggests that reports of Marconi's achievements had been received with some scepticism in the USA:

From time to time there has appeared in the technical journals a reference to the experiments showing the almost universal belief among electricians that, some day, wires will be done away with. Experiments have been made attempting to prove the possibilities, but it has remained for Mr Nikola Tesla to advance a theory, and experimentally prove it, that wireless communication is a possibility and by no means a distant possibility ... the principles involved have nothing in them to prevent messages being transmitted and intelligibly received between distant points. Already he has constructed both a transmitting apparatus and an electrical receiver.

Tesla's apparatus was already in existence, but had probably not then been shown to transmit Morse signals. Patent specifications were filed for the details of this system in September 1897.[37] Tesla's initial public display of the apparatus was spectacular — the operation of a remotely-controlled boat in a specially-installed tank of water at

Madison Square Garden − but it did not take place until a year later, in September 1898. This was not, however, the first public demonstration of radio in the USA. A Marconi set was exhibited to a meeting of the American Institute of Electrical Engineers in New York City on 15 December 1897.[38]

When Marconi arrived in Britain in 1896, he was just an unknown foreigner. He hoped − like Bell and the Bretts before him − to interest the British government in a new telegraphic device. Within a year he was to be one of the best-known applied scientists in the world. The first radio company was founded in 1897 to market his invention. Radio was no longer just a phenomenon with potential practical uses. It was the basis of a commercial industry.

Some commentators suggested, at the time and since, that Preece played an important part in the creation of that industry. He had been first, at the British Association meeting in 1896, to make a public announcement of Marconi's work. Later, during a lecture at the Toynbee Hall in December 1896, he was reported as saying that '... the Post Office had decided to spare no expense in experimenting with the apparatus'. It looked, from the accounts in the public press, as though Preece, almost alone among the country's leading telegraph engineers, was giving unqualified support to Marconi's efforts.

But the public press did not reveal the attitudes and decisions that were recorded in the Post Office's files. Preece, an experienced civil servant with many years in public office, was adept at revealing only what he wanted the public to know. There was no change in the established Post Office policy towards new inventions. Marconi was to have no more success than any other 'outsider' offering a new method of communication to the State's telegraph service.

References

1   B. L. Jacot and D. M. B. Collier, *Marconi, Master of Space*, London, Hutchinson, 1935, p. 199.

2   C. Trebilcock, *The Industrialization of the Continental Powers*, London, Longman, 1981, p. 341.

3   Jacot and Collier, *Marconi*, p. 24.

4   A. Righi, 'Su alcuno disposizioni speriementali per lo dimonstrazlione e lo studio delle ondulazioni di Hertz', *Il Nuovo Cimento*, XXXV, 1894, pp. 12−17.

5   Captain H. B. Jackson to Vice Admiral Sir John Fisher, 28 November 1900 (PRO, ref. ADM 116/570).

6 H.B. Jackson to C-in-C, Devonport, 16 September 1896 (PRO, ref. ADM 116/534).

7 O.J. Lodge, *Past Years*, London, Hodder & Stoughton, 1931, p. 232.

8 *Ibid.*

9 J.A. Fleming, *Principles of Electric Wave Telegraphy*, London, Longmans, 1906, p. 428.

10 G. Marconi to W.H. Preece, 10 November 1896 (MARCONI, file HIS 63).

11 British Patent Specification No. 12,039 of 1896, p. 2.

12 D. Paresce-Marconi, *My Father Marconi*, Wimbledon, Muller, 1962, p. 32.

13 Trebilcock, *Industrialization of Continental Powers*, p. 311.

14 K. Geddes, *Guglielmo Marconi: 1874–1937*, London, The Science Museum, 1974, p. 6.

15 A.A. Campbell Swinton to W.H. Preece, 30 March 1896 (PO, file ENG 23109).

16 British Patent Specification No. 5,028 of 1896.

17 A.A. Campbell Swinton, 'Electric currents of high pressure and periodicity', *Professional Papers of the Corps of Royal Engineers*, XXI, 1895, pp. 27–34.

18 G. Marconi to the Secretary of State for War, 20 May 1896 (PRO, ref. WO 32/989, file 84/M/3975).

19 C. Penrose to Inspector of Submarine Defences, 20 June 1896 (PRO ref. WO 32/989, file 84/M/3975).

20 'Statement of Captain Jackson's Claims as Regards the Invention of Wireless Telegraphy', appended to a letter, Captain F.T. Hamilton to the C-in-C, Devonport, 28 January 1899 (PRO, ref. ADM 116/523).

21 *The Times*, 23 September 1896.

22 O.J. Lodge to W.H. Preece, 16 October 1896 (IEE, Preece papers, SC Ms 22/213).

23 O.J. Lodge, 'The history of the Coherer principle', *The Electrician*, XL, 1897, pp. 87–91.

24 Lodge, *Past Years*, p. 232.

25 *The Electrician*, XXXIX, 1897, pp. 686–7.

26 *Daily Chronicle*, 20 September 1897.

27 G.M. Minchin, 'Wireless telegraphy', *The Electrician*, XXXIX, 1897, p. 832.

28 R. Appleyard, 'Wireless telegraphy', *The Electrician*, XXXIX, 1897, p. 869.

29 H. Benest, 'Wireless telegraphy', *The Electrician*, XL, 1897, p. 133.

30 A.A. Campbell Swinton, 'Wireless telegraphy', *The Electrician*, XXXIX, 1897, p. 869.

31 J.N.C. Kennedy, 'Wireless telegraphy', *The Electrician*, XL, 1897, pp. 22–3.

32 H.B. Jackson to G. Marconi, 29 May 1898 (MARCONI, file HIS 64).

33 A.T. Rawles, 'Jackson of the "Defiance"', *Journal of the Royal Naval Scientific Service*, IX, 1954, pp. 239–42.

34 British Patent Specification No. 11, 575 of 1897.

35   C. Süsskind, 'Popov and the beginnings of radiotelegraphy', *Proceedings of the Institute of Radio Engineers*, L, 1962, p. 2040.

36   *Electrical Review*, 9 July 1897.

37   US Patent Specifications Nos. 645,576 and 649,621 of 1897.

38   Anon., 'The Marconi system of wireless telegraphy', *The Electrician*, XL, 1897, p. 334.

PART III

Manufacture and marketing

Chart of principal events, July 1897 – September 1900

	Marconi Group	Royal Navy	General Post Office	Others
1897				
Jly	Wireless Telegraph & Signal Co. Signal Co registered			Lodge-Muirhead demonstration in London
Aug				
Sep				
Oct				
Nov			Dover radio trials	
Dec	GPO advise the Wireless Telegraph & Signal Co. that radio is not yet considered to be a practical system			Slaby's lecture in Berlin Ducretet's exhibition in Paris
1898				
Jan	Alum Bay station in operation			Marconi apparatus displayed in New York
Feb				
Mar				
Apr				
May	Royal Navy's Signals Committee visit Alum Bay			
Jun	Rathlin Island trials for Lloyds	Environmental trials of radio sets of HMS *Defiance*		Slaby-Arco radio department set up by AEG
Jly	Radio installed in Royal Yacht			
Aug				
Sep				
Oct				Tesla's demonstration in New York
Nov	Wireless Telegraph & Signal Co. request a GPO licence			
Dec	Radio installed in E. Goodwin lightship			

1899		
Jan		
Feb		
Mar	Hamilton's report on the *Defiance* radio trials Preece retires	
	Admiralty's first negotiations for the supply of radio apparatus	
Apr	Admiralty negotiations broken off when GPO start discussions with WT & Signal Co.	
May		
Jun		
Jly		Braun radio company registered
Aug	Marconi assists with Royal Navy's manoeuvres	
	Board of Admiralty recommend the adoption of radio	
Sep	Suspension of discussions between GPO and WT & Signal Co.	
Oct		
Nov	Royal Navy start building radio sets in HMS *Vernon*	
Dec	Unofficial talks between WT & Signal Co. and Admiralty	
1900		
Jan		Norddeutscher Lloyd purchase Marconi sets
Feb	Name changed to Marconi's Wireless Telegraph Co.	
Mar	Radio sets installed in ships on China and S. Africa stations	
	Marconi International Marine Co. registered	Radio workshop set up at Kronstadt by Popov for Russian Navy
Apr	GPO and Treasury approve resumption of Admiralty-Marconi negotiations	
May	Admiralty order for supply of Marconi apparatus	
Jun	*Vernon* sets perform badly during manoeuvres	
Jly		
Aug		
Sep	First batch of Marconi sets delivered to the Royal Navy	

9

Post Office dismissal

very interesting, but not encouraging   W. H. Preece, 1896

In the autumn of 1896, Preece was expressing support for Marconi's work in his public pronouncements – but he was recording a very different opinion in his departmental reports. The history of radio as suggested in the public press diverges abruptly from the history as revealed by the Post Office's files. Similarly, this narrative here diverges from most previous accounts of radio development. The contribution of the General Post Office – and of Preece in particular – has been over-emphasised in earlier works. Halsey,[1] for instance, says that 'Preece made no mistake ... but welcomed Marconi and gave full collaboration'. Eastwood[2] suggests that 'Marconi owed much to Preece's support'. Sturmey[3] describes Preece as being 'immediately interested', while Sharlin[4] says he was 'greatly impressed'. Aitken[5] claims that Preece 'acted quickly and with enthusiasm'. Jolly[6] writes of 'Preece's judgement in backing' Marconi.

This consensus of view among so many students of radio history is impressive, but it is mistaken. It is mistaken because it is based largely on accounts in the public press and on the reminiscences of early radio engineers (including Marconi himself) who relied on the public press for information on matters beyond their own direct experience. In this chapter, for the first time, evidence from the Post Office records is included to reveal the full, and very different, story.

Preece was not impressed by his first view of the Marconi apparatus, as demonstrated at the General Post Office in London in June 1896. P. R. Mullis, one of Preece's junior assistants, recalled, more than forty years later, that the equipment included

... a rather large-sized tubular bottle from which extruded two rods, terminating inside the bottle on two bright discs very close together and between which could be seen some bright filings or metal particles ... The curious glass tube (now spoken of as the coherer) was placed on a small table, and was joined in series with some batteries and a bell ... the key was depressed and immediately the bell on the adjacent table commenced and continued to ring. Marconi then went over to the glass tube and gave this a few sharp taps, when this bell ceased ringing ... The following day and the rest of the week were given over to further experimenting, which included putting a leather pad on the hammer of a heavier bell ... so that in action it automatically was brought into contact with the coherer and 'de-cohered' it.[7]

Despite the time that had elapsed before Mullis committed these memories to paper, they are consistent with a contemporary Post Office report which described the Marconi system as 'home made and somewhat crude appliances'.[8] The receiver was very primitive. A coherer in a 'large-sized tubular bottle' was not the same thing as the much smaller device described in Marconi's patent specification – and, moreover, it was shown to Preece on that first day without any mechanism for automatic de-coherence.

Marconi managed a much better display a month later, when, in the presence of several senior officials, he signalled from the roof of the General Post Office at St Martins le Grand to the roof of the Savings Bank in Knightrider Street. This display had two important results. One was a decision by Preece to arrange for more extensive tests on Salisbury Plain. The other was the meeting between Marconi and George Kemp (1857–1933), a Post Office technician who assisted with his experiments. A retired petty-officer instructor from the Royal Navy's torpedo schools, Kemp was to bring both a craftsman's skills and a devoted personal loyalty to Marconi's service for thirty-seven years.[9]

The trials on Salisbury Plain took place in September 1896. This was a few weeks after the War Office meeting, where Penrose and Carr were so impressed by the Marconi telegraph as to report that 'this application of the invention is capable of considerable further development without the apparatus becoming too cumbersome for military purposes. It is understood that the GPO are experimenting with the subject and it appears therefore unnecessary for the War Office to conduct experiments at present.'[10] Jackson, however, was not content to leave the trials to another department and arranged independently with Marconi to attend on Salisbury Plain as the Admiralty's representative. Kempe (that is, Preece's assistant, Harry Kempe, *not* George Kemp) was present on behalf of the Post Office.

The system was worked over ranges of about four kilometres in varying weather conditions. This was a considerable improvement over anything achieved in London, but still no better than the Post Office's own inductive system. No aerials were used in these experiments, the transmitter spark-gap and receiving coherer being at the foci of parabolic copper reflectors 'somewhat like a searchlight projector', according to Jackson's description.[11] Anxious to persuade Preece that the Salisbury Plain results did not represent the limits of the system's performance, Marconi wrote to the Post Office suggesting that aerials should be fitted in any future tests.[12]

But it seems that Preece had already made up his mind. Although Kempe had reported favourably on the trials (a copy of his comments[12] being subsequently forwarded to the army), his recommendations were rejected by Preece in a note appended to the first draft of the document: 'The report is interesting but not encouraging. I think our plan of using electro magnetic waves is cheaper and more practical ... It is amusing to find the War Dept waking up to a system of signalling without wires which we have been working at for nearly ten years!'[14] Two days after recording this adverse decision, Preece made his first announcement of the existence of Marconi's wireless telegraph to the British Association at Liverpool. He did not tell them that he had already decided that his department would not be using the system. The wording of his announcement led his audience to assume that, in this instance, traditional Post Office policy was being modified in favour of an 'outsider's' invention.

Preece may well have misled his audience deliberately. There was no reason why he should not have told the British Association that he had in effect rejected the Marconi telegraph. He reinforced the impression that the Post Office were encouraging Marconi's experiments with further statements to receptive audiences. During a public lecture at the Toynbee Hall on 12 December 1896, as reported in the *Westminster Gazette*, 'Mr Preece said that he had had the greatest possible pleasure in telling Mr Marconi ... that the Post Office had decided to spare no expense in experimenting with the apparatus.'[15] As one of Preece's biographers has remarked, '"spare no expense" was rhetorical. No Treasury authority had been sought for any such expenditure.'[16] Four months later, Marconi was advised by his solicitor (J. C. Graham) that such assistance as he had received from the Post Office did not put him under any obligation to the British government.[17] It may be inferred that this assistance was not on a very lavish scale.

Since, by the early autumn of 1896, Preece had concluded that the

Post Office would gain little from Marconi's work, it is surprising that he provided any assistance at all. Yet he did allow Marconi to use some of the Post Office's laboratory space and facilities. Baker, in his history of the Marconi organisation, suggests that

Preece had a perfectly sound reason for keeping a close eye upon this new means of communication ... If wireless telegraphy proved to be a success it could, if left to develop as a discrete and unsupervised entity, grow up to be a thorn in the GPO flesh. Preece, as a faithful servant of his organisation, was taking no chance on this happening..So in his close liaison with Marconi, Preece was able to give every opportunity for the new system of communication to show its paces and at the same time to maintain the closest awareness of every new technical development, on the age-old principle that to be forewarned is to be forearmed.[18]

Preece was following the policy which Graves had originally defined when offered Bell's telephone in 1877: committing the Post Office neither to accept the new invention nor to invest substantial sums in its development. But, at the same time, he had learned from his experience as Graves's deputy in the 1870s and subsequently that it might be unwise to ignore new technological developments altogether.

This method of monitoring Marconi's progress was not, however, put to very good use in practice. A further series of trials on Salisbury Plain during March 1897 provided the first opportunity in Britain to judge what improvements could be made by adding aerials to the radio system. Its range was increased spectacularly, consistently good signals being received over distances of eight kilometres. These results were reported by Jackson to the naval authorities and are recorded by entries in Kemp's personal diary[19] from 15 March to 25 March, 1897.[20] Yet there was no Post Office representative (except for Kemp, who was not in an influential post) present to witness this important technical development. In fact, a formal letter from the Post Office on 16 March 1897 advised the War Office that no wireless telegraphy experiments had been carried out since the previous September and the next trials would take place that summer near Cardiff.[21] Preece had presumably decided that an 'outsider' was unlikely to be doing anything worth serious investigation.

A new kind of radiation?

It seems strange that Preece should have troubled to set up a means of keeping in touch with Marconi's work and then to have ignored it. One reason, at least, may have been that he was more interested in the possibility that Marconi was investigating a new phenomenon than he was in the chance of acquiring a wireless telegraph. Preece thought that the Italian was working with a hitherto-unknown kind of radiation; he could have been making sure that this impressive scientific discovery would eventually be announced by the Civil Service from the Post Office's laboratories, and not by an academic physicist like Lodge nor by an independent consultant like Tesla.

The first tentative suggestion that novel effects might be observed in Marconi's experiments was made in the editorial columns of *The Electrician*. Commenting on the first series of Salisbury Plain trials in the autumn of 1896, the writer remarked that 'further technical information is unobtainable just now', and that 'Signor Marconi must have made a radically new departure in the "coherers" if the apparatus now enshrouded in mystery and hidden away on Salisbury Plain has been made reliable. So far "coherers" have been a trifle capricious in their behaviour.'[22] Preece himself then appeared to confirm this idea that Marconi had discovered unpublished secrets. At his Toynbee Hall lecture in December 1896, as reported in the *Westminster Gazette*:

Mr Preece announced that a Mr Marconi, a young Italian electrician, came to him recently with a system of telegraphy without wires, depending not on electro-magnetic but on electrostatic effects ... The great difference between the system which had already been tried [the inductive telegraph] and Mr Marconi's system was that in the former a wire on each side was necessary, and in the latter no wire was required.[23]

Preece evidently believed that the addition of parallel aerials at transmitter and receiver introduced an element of electromagnetic induction, so that the radio system then would offer no advantage over the Post Office's own wireless telegraph. Conversely, he thought that when the system were used without aerials its performance (although inferior) was due to some previously untried electrostatic phenomenon. This idea may have derived from Tesla's proposal to signal by transmitting waves through the earth's electrostatic field, though Marconi expected to utilise this effect *only* when aerial and earth connections were added at transmitter and receiver. Kemp, presumably paraphrasing what he understood to be Marconi's explanation of the phenomenon, recorded the reason for the improvements associated with aerials as '... you give the + charge to the plate and − charge to the Earth and the higher you have these plates the greater will be the potential as you have separated the two charges and consequently the greater distance you can work your Receiver'.[24] But if Preece believed that the essential feature of the 'electrostatic' method was that 'no wire was required', then he was not accepting Marconi's explanation in its entirety. For that matter, there was no real reason why he should have thought that any new effects were involved. Campbell Swinton had told him that the system used Hertzian waves, and there were practising engineers like Popov and Jackson who understood that the action of radio aerials was consistent with Maxwell's theory. Indeed, in March 1897, Jackson wrote to Marconi predicting, correctly, that the latter would eventually dispense with elevated metal plates at his aerials,' as the length of wire seems to me of much more importance'.[25]

The idea that a mysterious new radiation was responsible for Marconi's results persisted in some technical journals until the spring of 1897. *The Engineer*, a practically-oriented magazine which had consistently supported Preece in his disputes with Heaviside and Lodge, published an editorial article in its issue of 12 March 1897 which again accepted Preece's account of events and so helped to reinforce such misconceptions as already existed:

Nor is Mr Marconi's work being done in absolute privacy; on the contrary Mr W. H. Preece has, it is stated, been working with him, and results have already been attained which are not only startling in themselves but justify the belief that they are but the forerunner of astonishing developments of phenomena ... Signor Marconi produces the waves, but he cannot concentrate them in one direction. He has found that reflectors and receivers are worthless in the sense that he cannot direct rays in one path only.[26]

A year after Marconi came to Britain, and six months after his work had first been publicised at the British Association, some interested engineers still had no idea of how his equipment worked or what it had achieved.

The Lavernock radio trials

It was not until the early summer of 1897, after the Cardiff trials which had been mentioned in the Post Office's letters to the War Office, that it became generally understood that no new kind of radiation was involved. These trials simulated the conditions which might be experienced when signalling to an offshore lighthouse or lightship; the transmitter was installed on the coast at Lavernock Point, southwest of Cardiff, while the lightship was represented by the small island of Flatholm. Kemp supervised the work at both terminals, erecting not only the Marconi equipment but also a set of Preece's inductive telegraph apparatus, while Marconi and Preece welcomed representatives of the Royal Commission on Lightship Communication along with other invited observers.

The presence of so many influential visitors might have been an embarrassment. At the start of the trials, on Monday, 10 May 1897, the inductive system transmitted intelligible signals between Lavernock and Flatholm while Marconi tried unsuccessfully to emulate its performance. But on the Thursday he took his transmitter down onto the beach to increase its effective aerial length. The signal strength was much better with this new arrangement. As Kemp noted:

I started at 7 a.m. and fitted a new copper earth wire in lieu of the iron earth. I sent and received good signals on both systems between 12 and 12.45 p.m. The first half hour of V's were on a paper strip on the inker; the second 'so be it, let it be so' and the third 'it is cold here and the wind is up'.[27]

On the next day, these experiments were repeated to test the effects of minor circuit changes. The observers, satisfied that the previous day's success had been no accident, left the site to report to their employers.

Marconi and his assistants stayed at Cardiff, spending the weekend preparing for an attempt to signal across the Bristol Channel to Brean Down – a distance of fourteen kilometres. On Tuesday 18 May, transmissions from Lavernock Point were received successfully there throughout the afternoon. This particular trial achieved the greatest range of any system of wireless telegraphy to date. Kemp's diary – the only detailed source of information about these later trials – is rather vague after 27 May. It is evident, however, that the apparatus was dismantled and the whole party returned to London on Sunday, 30 May 1897.

The results of the Lavernock trials were reported to the Post Office, the army, and the Royal Navy as evidence of the practical value of the Marconi system. For those, such as Preece, who were not aware of the work on Salisbury Plain in the spring, the improvement in performance must have seemed almost unbelievable. This improvement was clearly due to the use of aerials, and, in particular, to the lengths of the aerial wires as suggested by Jackson. So the results contributed to a better understanding of the scientific principles involved. Marconi later commented to the Institution of Electrical Engineers that although he had once supposed that 'the electric oscillations are transmitted to the earth', he had since changed his mind and did 'not wish to say that I hold entirely to this view at present'.[28] Preece, too, had a better understanding of the system's principles of operation. He described the Lavernock experiments during a Friday Evening Discourse to the Royal Institution[29] with such clarity that an editorial writer in *The Electrician* was subsequently able to state with confidence that 'we have not to do with a new ether and a new "force" as the paragraphs in the daily Press might have led the unsophisticated to infer'.[30] Instead, the writer continued, Marconi's methods were the same as those already demonstrated by Lodge, though the Italian had achieved far greater ranges than Lodge had expected. This improved performance, it was suggested, could be attributed to an increase in wavelength. Lodge had generated waves of eight inches' length (20·3 cm), while Marconi used a wavelength estimated at forty-eight inches (121·9 cm, corresponding to a transmitter frequency of about 250 MHz).

Formation of the Wireless Telegraph and Signal Company

Preece's discourse at the prestigious Royal Institution, followed a fortnight later by a presentation to the yet-more-prestigious Royal Society, helped reinforce the popular impression that he had made significant contributions to Marconi's success. And, indeed, Preece had changed his mind as to the wisest official policy. In his formal report on the Lavernock trials, he recommended to the Secretary of the Post Office that the government should consider paying up to £10,000 for the patent rights to the Marconi system, provided that the Attorney General believed the patent to be legally valid.[31]

But this change of mind came too late. Preece had by then already shown that he was not always acting in Marconi's best interests.

Indeed, the Italian inventor believed that Preece had betrayed his trust to a potential rival. This rival, the German physicist Adolf Slaby (1849–1913), had been invited to the Lavernock trials at the request of Gisbert Kapp (born in Austria, a naturalised British subject, and then working as an electrical engineer in Germany). Kapp had written to Preece:

My friend, Privy Councillor Slaby ... is the private scientific adviser of the Emperor. Any new invention or discovery interests the Emperor and he always asks Slaby to explain it to him. Lately the Emperor has read of your and Marconi's experiments (the account got into a German paper from the *Strand* magazine) and he wants Slaby to report on this invention. Slaby has just been to see me and asked me to write to you on his behalf ... I shall be obliged if you will kindly answer the following questions.

(1) Is there anything in Marconi's inventions?
(2) If yes, could you arrange for Slaby and myself to see the apparatus and witness experiments if we came over to London towards the end of next week?

As the Emperor is in a hurry to get Slaby's report, will you kindly let me have a line by return? Please treat this letter as confidential and say nothing to Marconi about the Emperor.[32]

This letter was written on 19 March 1897, and must have been received in London during the second series of Salisbury Plain trials. As these trials were not noted by any of the Post Office senior staff, the Marconi system was presumably considered to be of no great practical value. Preece was more anxious to extend a courtesy to the German monarch than (despite the implicit warning in the final sentence of Kapp's letter) he was to protect commercial secrets which he regarded as having little importance. Marconi was less willing to invite Slaby to the demonstration, complaining later that

This gentleman, who was a professor at the Charlottenberg Technical Institute, came to England with introductions to the British Post Office authorities and at the request of Mr Preece, though very much against my own inclination, he was allowed to assist at these experiments and to observe all the details of the apparatus and methods employed.[33]

On the Thursday of the trials – the first day on which Marconi's apparatus worked effectively – Preece instructed Kemp to provide a spare set of the radio apparatus for Slaby's examination.[34] Returning to Germany, Slaby wrote to Preece that he had then '... constructed the whole apparatus of Mr Marconi and it works quite well'.[35] These experiments by Slaby started the work which led eventually to the foundation of Telefunken. In other words, the German radio industry can be said to have developed ultimately from Marconi's invention through the co-operation of the British post office. As the Telefunken group became Marconi's principal commercial rivals during the early twentieth century, it may be concluded in retrospect that his concern over Slaby's presence at Lavernock was justified.

After the Lavernock trials, Marconi knew that Preece had revealed his methods to another engineer. He was not aware, at the time, of Preece's confidential recommendation that the Post Office should consider purchasing the rights to the radio patent. But he was aware that others were interested in the commercial possibilities of his wireless telegraph. Jameson Davis had been actively canvassing support among his own contacts, and had offers of financial help from the Jameson family, the Davis family and their friends the Saunders and the Ballentynes. A week before the Lavernock trials, Jameson Davis drafted an agreement offering Marconi £15,000 in cash and 60,000 of his proposed Company's authorised capital of 100,000 £1 shares in return for the radio patent rights.[36] This was a very attractive proposition. Marconi nevertheless doubted the wisdom and propriety of accepting it while he was still associated with the Post Office, and protested to Preece 'that I have never sought these offers, or given encouragement to the promoters'.[37] He received little sympathy from Jameson Davis, who complained to his solicitors about the 'unbusinesslike' attitude of Marconi during these commercial negotiations.[38] All the same, Marconi persuaded his cousin to postpone the final decision until after the Lavernock trials.[39] And by then, Marconi had another excuse for prevarication, if he still felt that he needed one; he was invited to demonstrate his telegraph to the Italian Navy, and obliged in consequence to leave Britain temporarily.

Marconi had left Italy as an unknown and none-too-well qualified young man. He returned as a national hero, heralded by the Press, treated with deference by senior civil servants and naval officers, summoned to an audience with the King. The contrast with his treatment by the British Post Office, who welcomed him politely but then kept him waiting for more than a year without even, in Preece's words, letting him know that his system was 'considered ... a practical one',[40] must have been dramatic. He was reassured that there were other markets for his invention. Further, he could make sure that any new customers would not betray his confidence; his letters to

Jameson Davis after the Lavernock trials no longer argued for his obligation to Preece, but instead (prompted in part by his father[41]) insisted that he must retain control of his own invention. Having been reassured on this point, Marconi agreed to accept Jameson Davies's offer. He wrote from Italy to tell Preece of his decision:

The agreement [is] an exceedingly favourable one for me. Many other motives have also induced me to close. The first is that although the experiments have been very successful, yet the apparatus must be constructed in a more practical form and also extensive experiments must be undertaken. I have also felt that the business is too large for myself alone, as all the Governments in Europe want experiments carried out. The expense on Patents is also too much for me, especially as I must Patent some further improvements. This added to the great uncertainty of the life of the patents and to the vigorous opposition made to me by G. Lodge [sic] in England, Tesla in America and others in Europe have induced me to take this step.[42]

Marconi emphasised his financial difficulties in this letter. He was still without a regular salary at an age when he would normally have expected to be earning his own living. He was not aware that there was any prospect of receiving money from the Post Office, and a position as director of a manufacturing company would provide the dignity of an earned income (even although this income was derived, in the early days of the company, directly from his mother's relations).

With Marconi's signature on their agreement, Jameson Davis registered The Wireless Telegraph and Signal Company Ltd in London on 20 July 1897. Jameson Davis was himself the first managing director with Henry Allen as Company Secretary, and Marconi also serving on the Board.

Preece was surprised by Marconi's letter. He does not appear to have taken the Italian inventor's earlier concerns very seriously. His report on the Lavernock trials claimed confidently that Marconi could not make much progress without further Post Office assistance.[43] He retorted sharply to Marconi's news:

I was very sorry to get your letter. You have taken a step that I fear is very inimical to your personal interests. I regret to say that I must stop all experiments and all actions until I learn the conditions that are to determine the relations between your Company and the Government Departments who have encouraged and helped you so much.[44]

But if Preece believed that this reaction would eventually force the new company to accept whatever terms the Post Office might offer, then he was mistaken. There was already another potential customer interested in the Marconi system of wireless telegraphy. Advised by Jackson, the Royal Navy recognised that this apparatus might well provide a solution to their own communications problem.

References

1 R.J. Halsey, 'Britain's contribution to telecommunications', *Electronics and Power*, XIV, 1968, p.357.

2 E. Eastwood, 'Marconi, pioneer of wireless telegraphy', *Electronics and Power*, XX, 1974, p.309.

3 S.G. Sturmey, *The Economic Development of Radio*, London, Duckworth, 1958, p.17.

4 H.I. Sharlin, *The Making of the Electrical Age*, New York, Abelard-Schuman, 1963, p.92.

5 H.G.J. Aitken, *Syntony and Spark – the Origins of Radio*, New York, John Wiley, 1976, p.181.

6 W.P. Jolly, *Marconi*, London, Constable, 1974, p.38.

7 P.R. Mullis to 'Mr Faulkner', 20 October 1940 (MARCONI, file HIS 62).

8 J. Gavey, 'Report of Engineer-in-Chief of Post Office on Technical Aspect of Wireless Telegraphy' (PO, file Eng. 26411/03).

9 Kemp's account of the experiments on the GPO roof is in a manuscript notebook entitled 'G.S. Kemp – Diary of Wireless Expts at GPO and Salisbury 1896 and 1897' (MARCONI, file HIS 64).

10 C. Penrose and G. Carr, 'Signor Marconi's inventions' (PRO, ref. WO 32/989, file 84/M/3975).

11 H.B. Jackson to the C-in-C, Devonport, 16 September 1896 (PRO, ref. ADM 116/523).

12 G. Marconi to W.H. Preece, 10 November 1896 (MARCONI, file HIS 63).

13 H.R. Kempe, 'Signalling Across Space by Marconi's System', 20 September 1896 (PRO, ref. WO/989, file 84/M/4009).

14 W.H. Preece, note appended to the report of the Salisbury Plain trials, 20 September 1896 (PO file E 23109/1899, file 2).

15 *Westminster Gazette*, 14 December 1896.

16 E.C. Baker, *Sir William Preece, FRS: Victorian Engineer Extraordinary*, London, Hutchinson, 1976, p.268.

17 J.C. Graham to G. Marconi, 19 April 1897 (MARCONI, file HIS 43).

18 W.J. Baker, *A History of the Marconi Company*, London, Methuen, 1970, p.30.

19 References to entries in Kemp's diary are to the typewritten copy prepared by Kemp himself shortly before his death in 1933 and now in the Marconi archives. The manuscript original is still (to the best of my knowledge) held by Kemp's family and has not been made available for study.

20 Kemp's diary, 15–25 March 1897.

21 War Office – General Post Office correspondence, 2–16 March 1897 (PO, file ENG. 26173/1903).

22   *The Electrician*, XXXVII, 1896, p. 685.

23   *Westminster Gazette*, 14 December 1896.

24   G. S. Kemp, 'Diary of wireless expts at GPO and Salisbury 1896 and 1897' (MARCONI, file HIS 64).

25   H. B. Jackson to G. Marconi (undated) (MARCONI, file HIS 64).

26   Anon., 'The ether and its work', *The Engineer*, LXXXIII, 1897, p. 271.

27   Kemp's diary, 13 May 1897.

28   G. Marconi, 'Wireless telegraphy', *Proc. Inst. Elctr. Eng.*, XXVIII, 1899, p. 284.

29   W. H. Preece, 'Signalling through space without wires', *Proc. R. Inst.*, XV(ii), 1897, pp. 467–70.

30   *The Electrician*, XXXIX, 1897, p. 207.

31   W. H. Preece to Secretary of the Post Office, 15 July 1897 (PO, file E23109/99).

32   G. Kapp to W. H. Preece, 19 March 1897 (IEE, Preece papers, SC Ms 22/183).

33   The unpublished 'De Sousa Manuscript', in the MARCONI archives.

34   Kemp's diary, 13 May 1897.

35   A. Slaby to W. H. Preece, 27 June 1897 (IEE, Preece papers, SC Ms 22/177).

36   Draft agreement between G. Marconi and H. Jameson Davis, 30 April 1897 (MARCONI, file HIS 43).

37   'G. Marconi to W. H. Preece, 10 April 1897 (PO, file E 23109/1899).

38   H. Jameson Davis to Morten, Cutler and Co., 14 April 1897 (MARCONI, file HIS 43).

39   H. Jameson Davis to G. Marconi, 27 April 1897 (MARCONI, file HIS 43).

40   W. H. Preece to Secretary of the Post Office, 15 July 1897 (PO, file E 23109/1899).

41   D. Paresce-Marconi, *My Father Marconi*, Wimbledon, Muller, 1962, pp. 51–2.

42   G. Marconi to W. H. Preece, 27 July 1897 (MARCONI, file HIS 43).

43   W. H. Preece to Secretary of the Post Office, 15 July 1897 (PO, file E 23109/1899).

44   W. H. Preece to G. Marconi, 6 August 1897 (MARCONI, file HIS 43).

10

Military interest

I consider the system is worthy of a trial

Captain H.B. Jackson, RN, 1896

Early in the summer of 1899, readers of *The Times* were told that the Royal Navy's manoeuvres that year would 'be additionally interesting from the fact that experiments are to be made with the Marconi wireless telegraph'.[1] At about the same time, electrical engineers and others interested in the development of contemporary electrical signalling systems learned from Fahie's recently-published *A History of Wireless Telegraphy* that 'in December 1895 Captain Jackson, RN, commenced working ... and succeeded in getting Morse signals through space before he heard of Marconi. His experiments, however, were treated as confidential at the time, and have not been published.'[2] These short statements were all that most people knew of the preceding three years' naval research. The details of these researches, being recorded in documents with high security classifications, were revealed only to a few specialist naval officers and their civilian advisers. Such reticence is in marked contrast to Preece's assiduous, if selective, publicity-seeking. As a result, while the work of the Post Office has been over-emphasised in many histories of radio, the very important contribution of the Royal Navy has generally been neglected.

Jackson's appreciation of Marconi's work

It was not only in their attitudes to publicity that these two departments' policies differed so noticeably. While the Post Office at first saw little use for radio, the Royal Navy had soon recognised its potential. Jackson first met Marconi at the War Office conference on 31 August 1896 and saw the Marconi wireless telegraph working under practical conditions on Salisbury Plain in the following month.

This was about the time when Preece decided that the Post Office had no need for radio telegraphy. But Jackson reported to his superiors in the Royal Navy that 'for military purposes, as an auxiliary signal for fog, and transmitting secret intelligence, its adoption would be almost invaluable ... for these reasons ... I consider the system is worthy of a trial'.[3] He also wrote personally to Marconi, saying that the radio apparatus '... is worth a trial, and would be of use to the service, if the signals can be made over three miles [5 kilometres]'.[4] Although this letter is worded rather more cautiously than Jackson's official report, it is nevertheless a firm expression of his interest. He was an experienced officer of senior rank, and understood the implications of such a commitment when writing on behalf of his service to a civilian inventor.

Clearly, Jackson was more enthusiastic than Preece about Marconi's invention. Indeed, by the conclusion of the Salisbury Plain trials he was already planning a further series of maritime tests for the Marconi telegraph. Jackson suggested that

the apparatus be first fixed up on the two torpedo boats attached to this school [HMS *Defiance*] for preliminary trial ... It should then be fitted to ships in commission for trial and report under service conditions. Three or more receivers ... should be included in the order (with one transmitter) to ascertain that they behave similarly under all conditions, and these could be eventually distributed amongst several ships of the squadron, the flaship alone having the transmitter.[5]

Although this same report emphasised that the Marconi apparatus 'would be invaluable for friendly torpedo boats to signal their approach', the proposed trial shows that Jackson's idea had expanded beyond the original concept of radio as a means of signalling between torpedo boats to include the wider problem of enabling an Admiral in his flagship to keep in touch with all ships under his command, even, in the words of Jackson's report, 'in a fog, and when the ships were not visible, or even aware of their proximity to each other'. This same requirement, of transmitting orders from a flagship to the commanders of subordinate vessels, prompted him to suggest to Marconi that apparatus for naval service should be designed to work 'without reflectors; all round lenses would be permissible'.[6] Such all-round performance was not needed when working between fixed terminals; reflectors would have been quite adequate for communication with lighthouses and lightships, as Preece envisaged.

In practice, the desired non-directional characteristic was imparted to the apparatus with aerials and not 'all round lenses'. Aerials were tried by Marconi during the second series of Salisbury Plain trials, from 15 March to 25 March 1897. Jackson, at Marconi's invitation, visited the site on 24 March and reported that the radio telegraph had been working consistently over ranges of eight kilometres and intermittently up to eleven kilometres. This performance, comparable with the best that had been achieved by inductive wireless telegraph systems, Jackson attributed to 'using wires insulated in the air, which were raised from the earth 60 to 120 feet by flying kites or balloons, and by connecting one pole of both transmitter and receiver to earth'. He also reported that he had, as a consequence of these trials, fitted aerial wires to the masts of HMS *Defiance*, and found that they made a marked improvement in the performance of his own apparatus.[7]

By the end of March 1897, therefore, the Royal Navy's torpedo officers were aware of the impressive increase in range that was possible in existing radio systems. They had, on Marconi's advice, incorporated the latest modifications into their own experimental equipment. It was to be nearly two more months before the Lavernock trials demonstrated the importance of these modifications so convincingly to the Post Office's engineering staff. Preece was then working in the same building as Marconi, but he knew less about Marconi's experiments than did Jackson, who was stationed over two hundred kilometres away!

Radio trials under service conditions

While experiments were taking place on Salisbury Plain, Jackson was considering how the Marconi apparatus might best be adapted for the more rigorous conditions to be expected at sea. His report in September 1896 had emphasised that the system was then 'still in the laboratory stage, and as such ... hardly fit for practical trial in HM Ships at sea'. He identified the main problems to be anticipated with radio sets in warships as

the use of the so-called high tension electricity in the form of a powerful induction coil, with the necessary high insulation required ... and the remote possibility of injurious effects (yet unknown) on the other circuits, fuses and compasses in the ship ... also the fact that, except under certain conditions, all receivers in the fleet would record every signal made by every ship (unless switched off), thus rendering it impossible for two ships to signal at once, or all ships to answer a general signal together.[8]

Jackson recommended that 'a design might well be prepared and made suitable for the roughest usage'. Accordingly, in the early months of 1897, he made such an apparatus, writing to Marconi that 'I tried my apparatus in heavy rain this morning, the transmitter being entirely exposed to the weather and all the braiding of the wires soaking wet, yet my results were very good and the signals were apparently quite unaffected by the wet wires.'[9] He then organised a series of tests such as he had proposed in the previous September, working the sets at sea between the torpedo craft attached to the *Defiance* establishment. The Commander-in-Chief at Devonport was invited formally to watch one such set of tests on 20 May 1897. With the transmitter in the gunboat HMS *Scourge* and the receiver on board HMS *Defiance*, signalling was demonstrated over various distances up to about five kilometres, sometimes with the transmitting vessel stationary and sometimes under way. Conditions in the harbour and the Lynher river prevented an attempt to determine the maximum range of the transmitter, but the observers were generally satisfied with the performance of the system. One especially important detail was the confirmation that Jackson had been correct when he predicted that large metal plates, as used by Marconi, would not be needed at the tops of the aerial wires. The existing masts of warships provided excellent supports for the aerials, much better than the kites and balloons which Marconi had used on Salibury Plain, while the ships' metal hulls were 'earthed' in the sea.

Jackson also used this apparatus to investigate some of the problems associated with the use of high voltages. He reported that

dangerous shocks are unobtainable ... it does not affect the 'Scourge's' compass, though within 10 feet of it; and though I have endeavoured to fire fuzes directly by its means, I have not succeeded in doing so, thus proving that it will not cause premature firing of guns or torpedoes 'at the ready' ... the various parts of the apparatus are not more delicate than other electrical instruments in the service, and ... require practically no more attention than them, when once adjusted.[10]

His direct involvement in the trials ended, however, that autumn when he completed his tour of duty in the training ship. The naval authorities did not extend his appointment beyond its usual term, nor would a prolonged period in such a specialised post have enhanced his prospects for promotion to Flag rank with its varied duties, and he was posted to the British Embassy in Paris as Naval Attache on 1 November 1897. Although he had established a reputation as an experimental applied scientist among his colleagues, his primary tasks as Captain of HMS *Defiance* had been the administration of his ship and the training of his subordinates. Jackson had discharged this latter responsibility so well that the radio experiments continued without interruption under the supervision of his successor, Captain F. T. Hamilton, RN.

The officers in HMS *Defiance*, advised sometimes by correspondence from Jackson, concentrated their efforts on improving the details of the radio transmitter and receivers for use at sea. Hamilton complained that 'this has presented great difficulties, as the instruments obtainable in the market are not such as readily adapt themselves to the somewhat rough conditions of the service afloat'.[11] Nevertheless, he made some progress during 1898, simplifying the transmitter, improving the reliability of the coherer circuit, and using non-absorbent materials for insulation wherever possible. He also considered it prudent to confirm some of Jackson's earlier findings by consulting Kelvin and Preece to verify that there were no particular dangers associated with the use of high-voltage induction coils in warships.

Relations between the Royal Navy and the Wireless Telegraph and Signal Company

Marconi had been encouraged to keep on with his work by the Royal Navy's interest during the time when the Post Office's engineers were ignoring his researches. He took Jackson's advice and developed his apparatus, especially by adopting aerial wires, in such ways as would make it most useful in ships at sea. No doubt, considering his own interests and ambitions, Marconi found that naval officers were congenial companions. But he had not received any direct instruction, nor any financial aid, from the Royal Navy. There was no support comparable with the Post Office's provision of laboratory facilities which might imply some claim on his loyalty. This proved to be no disadvantage; Marconi's personal relationship with the Royal Navy's officers was less restrained (and included more voluntary co-operation, such as his care to keep in touch with Jackson) than his relationship with the Post Office. With no formal commitment on either side, there was no reason for any change in this relationship between Marconi and his acquaintances in the Royal Navy after the formation of the Wireless Telegraph and Signal Company in the Summer of 1897.

Indeed, the new Company's first recorded radio trials, in December 1897, were much as might have been organised by the Royal Navy. A transmitter at the Needles Hotel, in the Isle of Wight, exchanged signals with a small steam tug in Alum Bay, at different ranges and bearings and in varying weather conditions. These experiments continued until the end of the year, by which time the ranges had been steadily increased to about thirty kilometres despite heavy seas, rain and fog.[12] Kemp, who had left the Post Office service to join the Wireless Telegraph and Signal Company in November 1897, assisted Marconi at these trials.[13]

Although some aspects of these Alum Bay trials were obviously applicable to communication with lighthouses and lightships, the overall plan with its emphasis on signalling to and from moving vessels in difficult weather was more directly related to the Royal Navy's needs. Without any formal policy decisions from its directors, the Company was investigating advanced applied science in order to solve defence problems. This situation was not, however, defined very clearly at the end of 1897. The Company received no direct payment from the Royal Navy for this research, and any findings would have been as applicable to merchant vessels as to warships.

Marconi kept in touch with the Royal Navy by correspondence and by inviting members of the Signals Committee to visit his station at the Needles Hotel in May 1898. The report written by the Committee's secretary after this visit summarises the technical progress which had been made since the formation of the Wireless Telegraph and Signal Company. It also reveals that senior naval officers were already considering the influence that this new means of signalling would have on traditional naval tactics. The problem, which Jackson had earlier identified, of mutual interference between the signals of two ships in a fleet which attempted to operate radio sets at the same time, might soon be solved, using 'an arrangement by which Signor Marconi says he is able to choke or regulate the vibrations (called "tuning" the instrument), so that only those instruments working at the same "tune" should be able to receive a message'. On the other hand, the risks of deliberate interference – later known as 'jamming' – were also recognised:

It seems possible ... for an enemy to spoil your communications by simply transmitting perpetual signs ... and convert all communications into a jumble. For instance, if a blockaded port had a transmitter, the communications of the blockaders (when you had once got their tune) could always be thrown out if in distance ... cruisers watching a channel ... would find their communications thrown out, when most needed, by the presence of hostile ships also using the system.[14]

The Committee's report concluded that the risk of jamming 'would show rather a reason for having the system in the service, than not, if only for the purpose of incommoding our possible enemies'. Marconi and his commercial advisers would have found this conclusion encouraging (if they ever learned of it), as it meant that a contract to supply radio sets to *any* navy in the world should enhance sales by attracting orders from possible adversaries. In the long run, the freedom to take advantage of such opportunities as they arose might well be more profitable than any agreement for government funding which also involved a restriction on foreign business.

By the beginning of 1899 signals and torpedo specialists within the Royal Navy had determined how radio might be used to solve several existing communications problems. The techniques had been developed originally (so far as the Royal Navy were concerned) as a method of signalling to and between fast torpedo boats. Subsequently, Jackson had suggested that radio apparatus would help an Admiral in his flagship to keep in touch with the individual ships of his squadron or fleet. Hamilton realised that improved communications might enable a limited number of scouting cruisers to patrol a much larger area of the oceans than would be possible when maintaining contact by visual signalling alone. He pointed out that 'it would immensely lengthen the distance to which a line of scouts could be thrown out at night or in thick weather'.[15] Finally, the Board of Admiralty decided to initiate what would be, in effect, the last phase of Jackson's proposed trials with 'three or more receivers ... distributed amongst several ships of the squadron'. They asked the Wireless Telegraph and Signal Company to quote for the supply of (at first) two sets of apparatus. The Company's managing director, Jameson-Davis, replied late in March, offering each set of transmitter and receiver for £59 11s 0d, plus an annual royalty of £100 for each installation.[16] At least one member of the Board commented that this proposed royalty was very high. But before this financial discussion could be completed, there was an interruption. Other government departments were also interested in the possible uses of radio telegraphy, though none had investigated the system to the same extent as the Royal Navy. The Post Office were again in contact with the Marconi directors. With the approval of the Treasury, the

Post Office had decided to discuss the terms on which the Company might agree to provide apparatus for any government purposes. The Royal Navy, which had an immediate need for Marconi apparatus, was instructed by Treasury officials to suspend its separate approach to the Company.[17] Instead, the Post Office – which, Preece claimed, did not need the Marconi telegraph, and still had identified no particular application for the system – would negotiate on their behalf.

References

1　*The Times*, 17 July 1899.

2　J.J. Fahie, *A History of Wireless Telegraphy*, Edinburgh, Blackwood, 1899, p.202.

3　Captain H.B. Jackson to C-in-C, Devonport, 16 September 1896 (PRO, ref. ADM 116/523).

4　H.B. Jackson to G. Marconi, 15 September 1896 (MARCONI, file HIS 64).

5　H.B. Jackson to C-in-C Devonport, 15 September 1896 (PRO ref. ADM 116/523).

6　H.B. Jackson to G. Marconi, 15 September 1896 (MARCONI, file HIS 64).

7　H.B. Jackson to C-in-C, Devonport, 31 March 1897 (PRO, ref. ADM 116/523).

8　H.B. Jackson to C-in-C, Devonport, 16 September 1896 (PRO, ref. ADM 116/523).

9　H.B. Jackson to G. Marconi, 19 May 1897 (MARCONI, file HIS 64).

10　H.B. Jackson to C-in-C, Devonport, 22 May 1897 (PRO, ref. ADM 116/523).

11　Captain F.T. Hamilton to C-in-C, Devonport, 28 January 1899 (PRO, ref. ADM 116/523).

12　G. Marconi, 'Wireless telegraphy', *Proc. Inst. Elec. Eng.*, XXVIII, 1899, p.288.

13　Kemp's diary, 19 November and 5–19 December 1897.

14　Commander H. Evan Thomas to the President of the Signal Committee, 10 May 1898 (PRO, ref. ADM 116/523).

15　F.T. Hamilton to C-in-C, Devonport, 28 January 1899 (PRO ref. ADM 116/523).

16　H. Jameson-Davis to the Secretary of the Admiralty, 29 March and 18 April 1899 (PRO, ref. ADM 116/523).

17　General Post Office to the Secretary of the Admiralty, 5 May 1899 (PRO, ref. ADM 116/523).

11

Civil service cynicism

... pure scientific apparatus 'boomed' by financial speculators for
their own individual gain.   *Nature*, 1899

The Royal Navy, one possible customer for Marconi equipment, had
co-operated constructively with the Wireless Telegraph and Signal
Company. Anxious to cultivate other potential customers, the
Company's directors tried to establish a similar co-operative relationship with the Post Office. At their first Board meeting in August 1897
they passed a formal resolution expressing their 'appreciation of Mr
Preece's friendly assistance in experimenting with the Marconi system
and their desire to continue in such friendly relationship with Her
Majesty's Government', and also suggested a meeting between their
solicitor and the Post Office's legal representatives to decide the basis
of this 'friendly relationship'.[1]

But they were already too late. While the civil servants in the Post
Office might prevaricate about technical decisions, they could act
promptly where matters of law and administration were concerned.
They had consulted their own advisers, even before receiving the
Company's resolution. Accepting Preece's version of events, the Post
Office's solicitor believed that the development of radio owed much
to Post Office financial and technical support. He advised therefore
that no assistance should be given to what he described as a 'private
money-making Association' unless it were in return for some direct
benefit to the Post Office – thereby confirming that the policy
towards new inventions as enunciated by Graves some twenty-two
years earlier was still considered appropriate. Further, any public
communications service offered by the Company itself would infringe
the Postmaster-General's monopoly of inland telegraphs. Almost as
an afterthought, the solicitor added that the Post Office would in any
case, be entitled to use Marconi's invention for their own purposes
under the provisions of Section 27 of the Patents, Designs and Trade

Marks Act of 1883.[2] At the time in 1897, the engineer-in-chief did not anticipate any need to use the Marconi apparatus. Two years later, however, his department would invoke the Patents Act exactly as their solicitor had suggested.

Within three days of receiving the solicitor's advice, the Secretary of the Post Office warned the engineering department that in future Marconi would not be allowed to assist at any Post Office wireless telegraphy trials, and that any negotiations involving Marconi were to treat him as a representative of his Company and not as a private individual.[3] Late in August 1897, Marconi sought an interview with Preece. The engineer-in-chief reported he had told the Italian inventor that all Post Office radio experiments were to be suspended until the Post Office had come to a definite understanding with the Company. In addition, he said, he had informed Marconi that they could no longer negotiate as individuals but only as employees of their respective organisations.[4] But Marconi's impression of this interview was rather different. He wrote to his father, describing Preece as being 'extremely kind to me, as always', and as saying that 'my having made a contract with the Company concerns myself only. If the Company continues to be friendly he will do all he can to forward my discovery … he thinks very soon the discovery will be taken up by the British Government who will come to an agreement with the Company.'[5] Marconi was, perhaps, repressing any doubts which he might have felt so as to reassure his father. Nevertheless, it appears that Preece's official reports and unofficial statements could still convey two different opinions.

Indeed, some people within the Post Office service itself may well have been misled by Preece's report. Despite what had been written, the Post Office's engineers did not immediately abandon all radio experiments. Instead, as explained by Preece's deputy, John Gavey, '… it was decided, instead of dropping the experiments at once, to carry on quite privately such part of the proposed programme as was justified by the arrangements already made'.[6] These arrangements, for trials of radio apparatus at Fort Burgoyne, near Dover, had been planned as a preliminary study for a permanent installation at the South Foreland lighthouse at a later date. The trials were carried out in three phases at various dates from mid-September to mid-October 1897. Jackson, observing the experiments for the Royal Navy, reported that the performance of the equipment was generally not so good as that achieved by Marconi. Preece himself confirmed this relatively poor performance, admitting that 'the results obtained at Dover are distinctly unfavourable, when compared with those we had between Lavernock and Brean Down'.[7]

These unsatisfactory results provoked Preece into a surprising reversal of his declared policy – he contacted Marconi and persuaded him to assist with the trials. Marconi visited Fort Burgoyne on 6 October, and there adjusted the Post Office apparatus to work over what proved to be the greatest range attained in the series of trials, but with shorter aerials and less power than the Post Office engineers had used. It was embarrassingly evident that Marconi's successes owed less to Post Office expertise than Preece had claimed, and this may well have been the reason why his contribution to the Dover experiments was largely ignored. For although Marconi's presence at these trials was recorded in his own letters[8] and in Jackson's report,[9] it was not mentioned at all in Preece's official account, while Gavey declared that the trials were 'conducted solely by the officers of the Department without the assistance or co-operation of Signor Marconi'.[10] These senior engineers apparently had no wish to advertise either their change in policy or their technical embarrassment to their superiors!

Having completed the Dover trials, the Post Office, at last, suspended further radio experiments. There was no positive attempt to reach the 'definite understanding' with the Wireless Telegraph and Signal Company which Preece had claimed to be his objective. Instead, the Company was told curtly that the Post Office considered that radio telegraphy 'could scarcely yet be regarded as having reached a practical stage'.[11]

Experimental installations for offshore telegraphy

Despite this discouraging judgement, it was evident by the end of 1897 that the Marconi radio system was the most effective means of wireless telegraphy which had then been devised. This was recognised by the members of the Royal Commission on Lighthouse Communication when they reported that the inductive wireless telegraph had proved unsuitable for lightships, 'the electrical energy being almost entirely lost in the sea', whereas the Lavernock trials had shown Marconi's system to be more satisfactory.[12] Considering that some kind of electrical communication with light-vessels was needed urgently, especially as it could be the means of saving lives from a collision near a lighthouse or lightship, the Commissioners had 'arranged for a practical trial of the Marconi system at a light-vessel'. The responsibility for organising this practical trial had been delegated to the Post Office's engineers; the Commissioners felt consequently that their own task was completed.

But the Post Office had abandoned their radio experiments after what were only preliminary trials at Fort Burgoyne. Practical trials of radio apparatus in maritime environments were confined to the Royal Navy's experiments and such tests as the Wireless Telegraph and Signal Company could arrange for the Marconi system in offshore service. Regular trials in various conditions were, of course, organised at the Company's station at Alum Bay. And there were further opportunities in May 1898 to study the performance of Marconi apparatus in regular operation. Lloyds had asked for a demonstration of a radio link between Ballycastle and their signal station at Rathlin Island, off the Irish coast. The Wireless Telegraph and Signal Company provided the necessary equipment with two assistants, Kemp and Glanville, to instal and work it.[13] This installation is described in the Company's history as 'entirely successful', ten ships being reported in the first month of operation, even although the visual signalling link was sometimes obscured by fog.[14] Lloyd's records, however, show that the performance of the Rathlin Island station was marred by a series of mishaps, the worst being the death of Glanville in an accidental fall from a cliff.[15] The installation was not as reliable as had been hoped, and it was eventually dismantled, at Lloyd's request, in September 1898.

Despite this setback, the Company still hoped to profit by supplying sets for lighthouses and lightships. They therefore arranged to demonstrate their equipment to the Trinity House authorities with a radio link between the East Goodwin lightship and the South Foreland lighthouse in Kent. Kemp, again, was put in charge of the actual installation and completed the work in a few days, despite bad weather. The first good signals were exchanged on Christmas Eve 1898, regular communications being maintained over the twenty kilometre range from then onwards. Marconi reported to the Institution of Electrical Engineers that 'various members of the crew learned in two days how to send and receive, and in fact how to run the station ... owing to the assistant on board not being as good a sailor as the instruments have proved ot be'. This rather unfair comment (Kemp, an experienced seaman, was suffering something more serious than ordinary seasickness, but stayed loyally on board the lightship until early in the New Year) was intended to convey the message that, contrary to the Post Office's opinion, radio was already simple and reliable enough for practical use. Referring again to the work of the lightship's crew, Marconi continued:

nearly all the messages during very bad weather are sent and received by these men, who, previous to our visit to the ship, had probably scarcely heard of wireless telegraphy, and were certainly unacquainted with even the rudiments of electricity. It is remarkable that wireless telegraphy, which had been considered by some as rather uncertain, or that might work one day and not the next, has proved in this case to be more reliable, even under such unfavourable conditions, than the ordinary land wires, very many of which were broken down in the storms.[16]

In effect, Marconi was telling the members of the Institution that his apparatus was more reliable than the land lines maintained by Preece and his colleagues in the Post Office service.

On 17 March 1899, the steamship *Elbe* went aground on the Goodwin Sands in thick fog; the lightship's crew used the Marconi apparatus to summon the Ramsgate lifeboat. A month later, the lightship was itself rammed by the *R. F. Matthews*, again during a fog. This accident, too, was reported by radio, though no immediate assistance was needed this time. Only four months after its first installation on board a lightship, radio was proving its worth in emergencies, precisely as members of the Royal National Lifeboat Institution and of the Royal Commission on Lighthouse Communication had predicted.

The appearance of rival companies

By early 1899, when Marconi presented his paper to the Institution of Electrical Engineers and extolled the reliability of his invention, there were already competitors anxious to secure contracts in the same market. Popov, for instance, had resumed his experiments for the Russian navy in the autumn of 1896, and had also made tentative moves towards the commercial exploitation of his researches. The initial impulse for commercial development seems not to have come from Popov himself but from Eugene Ducretet (1844–1908), a Parisian scientific-instrument manufacturer who wrote to Popov early in 1897 asking whether he might have anticipated Marconi in any respects. Popov's reply, largely concerned with the details of his lightning detector/radio receiver circuit, was apparently enough to satisfy Ducretet that the Marconi patent might be circumvented. On 19 November 1897 he displayed radio apparatus made by his own Company at an exhibition in Paris, with accompanying descriptions acknowledging the contributions of Hertz, Righi, Bose, Branly and Popov. Some French physicists later criticised this presentation for its blatant omission of Lodge and Marconi. Ducretet was no doubt attempting to establish that his system did not contravene the patents of Marconi and Lodge, the only important radio patents which had been filed by the autumn of 1897, and perhaps hinting that his association with Popov was itself a contribution to the Franco-Russian naval alliance.

There were other competitors in Germany. As Marconi had anticipated, Slaby continued his experiments with apparatus similar to that he had seen at Lavernock. On 1 November 1897, Slaby described some of these experiments in a lecture at Berlin.[17] The ranges achieved during these tests, up to twenty-one kilometres, were the best that had been recorded at the time by any experimenter other than Marconi. Despite generous tributes to the Italian's contribution, this lecture was itself evidence that there was a potential rival to the Marconi system being developed in Germany. In 1898 Slaby, with his assistant, Count Arco (1869–1940), formed a wireless telegraphy department within the powerful AEG electrical combine. A second German radio company was founded in July 1899, when Ferdinand Braun (1850–1918), Professor of Physics at the University of Strasbourg, registered 'Prof. Brauns Telegraphie GmbH', with the Siemens and Halske group as major shareholders.

But at the time Marconi was not unduly worried about the entry of these German electrical giants into the radio industry. His correspondence shows that he was more concerned with the immediate competition from Lodge and his supporters in Britain. After recommencing radio experiments in 1897, Lodge soon recognised the lack of any means of selective tuning as the main practical disadvantage of the Marconi system. He accordingly designed and patented a 'syntonised' wireless telegraph which enabled its operators

to change easily from one rate of oscillation to another, and thus signal first to one station and then to another, using the appropriate key for each station ... to the end that the electric oscillations purposely excited at a distant station in another syntonised circuit may excite in the first one a response.[18]

Lodge and Muirhead showed apparatus built to this design at a Royal Society soiree on 16 June 1897. Their company – the Lodge–Muirhead Syndicate – was not to be registered until 1901, but this display at the country's principal scientific institution was, for Marconi, disturbing evidence of collaboration between a well-known physicist and a leading manufacturer of telegraphic apparatus. His concern was justified, especially as Lodge's system already incorporated selective tuning circuits similar to those which Marconi was still developing at that period.

Aware of the potential competition from these rivals, the Wireless Telegraph and Signal Company were careful to publicise every one of their own minor successes. While they had yet to receive any substantial orders, several small contracts during 1898–99 provided opportunities to publicise the Company's work, especially when the presence of well-known scientists appeared to imply their approval of the technology. Lord Kelvin visited the Alum Bay station in June 1898. Fitzgerald was a passenger in the reporters' launch when the *Dublin Daily Express* used Marconi apparatus to transmit its correspondent's account of a regatta at Kingstown (now Dun Laoghaire). Best of all, as a source of favourable publicity, there was a Royal order for Marconi sets in July 1898; Queen Victoria, in Osborne House on the Isle of Wight, wished to keep in touch with her son, the Prince of Wales, who was convalescing on board the Royal Yacht.[19] Somewhat later, in September 1899, Marconi was again able to attract the attention of the press on a ship-board radio installation when he was invited to the USA to assist in reporting the America's Cup yacht races.[20]

By the summer of 1898, Marconi was already planning an even more spectacular demonstration – radio transmissions across the English Channel. This was technically feasible, but it could have been difficult getting permission to site a station on French soil. Political relations between Britain and France were severely strained, to such an extent that the Fashoda confrontation in the autumn provoked both naval commands into preparation of war plans and the mobilisation of some reserves. Marconi wrote to Jackson at the Paris embassy for advice. Jackson, appreciating the political problems, but apparently not understanding Marconi's wish to achieve the maximum possible publicity for the experiment, suggested instead 'why not try from the Isle of Wight to Portland Bill where you would have a free sea space of about forty-five miles and would have no

difficulty in getting permission'.[21] Despite this suggestion, the
Company persisted with its application. On 2 March 1899, Marconi
– who, by accident or design, was again able to arrange for his
announcement to be reported widely – told the Institution of
Electrical Engineers that 'the official consent of the French Government has ... been received this evening'.[22] There was already a
suitable British terminal for the experiment at the South Foreland
lighthouse. Equipment for the new French station was installed in the
Chalet d'Artois, Wimereux, near Boulogne. Marconi sent the first
radio signals from France to England on 27 March 1899, having first
made certain that representatives of the French government were
present to witness this historic event and ensure that it was reported
prominently in the press of both countries. The transmissions, of
course, included several formal messages of the kind usually considered appropriate to such occasions. But with three stations, at
Wimereux, the South Foreland and the East Goodwin lightship, in
relatively close proximity, Marconi also took the opportunity of
experimenting with various means of improving the selectivity in his
receivers to eliminate unwanted signals from nearby transmitters.

John Ambrose Fleming (1850–1945), Professor of Electrical
Technology at University College, London, visited the South Foreland
station soon after the start of cross-Channel transmissions.[23] He then
suggested to Marconi that the radio link could well be featured at the
British Association meeting in Dover that September. Alert, as usual,
to the possibility of more useful publicity, Marconi arranged a
demonstration which involved the exchange of greetings between the
British Association and similar meetings of scientific societies in
France and Italy, messages to the latter group being re-transmitted
over the landlines from Boulogne to Como. This was to be one of
the last important operations of the Wimereux station, which was shut
down and dismantled shortly afterwards.

The Company's financial prospects

Marconi had not over-estimated the publicity value of the cross-
Channel link. This first demonstration of international radio
telegraphy brought a rapid rise in the Company's quotation on the
stock market. One-pound shares reached a peak of more than seven
pounds for a short time, and remained above six pounds for several
months.[24] Some journalists contributed to this rise by prophesying

that the Marconi system would soon render both landlines and submarine cables obsolescent. But the increase in share prices did not correspond to an increase in lucrative business. There were hopes of orders from the Royal Navy, but no firm commitment beyond the enquiry about the supply of two sets for the 1899 annual manoeuvres. No dividend had yet been paid to the Company's investors, and none was to be paid in the near future. The energetic publicity campaign had been quite effective, but, as Baker remarks in the Company's history, 'the plaudits of onlookers ... do not pay shareholders' dividends and the order book was deplorably empty'.[25]

Financial problems were exacerbated by uncertainties about future policy. With no immediate prospect of orders from the Post Office, the Company hoped to exploit the offshore communications market by erecting shore stations to be operated by Trinity House, Lloyd's, or by the Company themselves. But, soon after the Kingstown regatta, they had been warned by the Post Office that 'the working of any systematic arrangement of this description would constitute an infringement of the Postmaster-General's exclusive telegraph rights'.[26] Evidently the Company directors thought it prudent to avoid any more such accusations. In December 1898, shortly before installing radio apparatus in the South Foreland lighthouse, they wrote to the Post Office requesting a licence for ship-to-shore communications. There was no response. The Post Office alone could not make a decision in a matter involving public finance. After some discussion, they referred the matter to the Treasury for further direction.

Failure of negotiations between the Company and the Post Office

This request for a licence had obliged the Post Office, at last, to reconsider their policy as regards radio telegraphy. The situation had changed considerably since their abrupt suspension of radio research late in 1897. For one thing, Preece had left the Post Office service in February 1899 on reaching the retirement age for civil servants. His successor, John Gavey, was less committed to the inductive wireless telegraph. More important, from Gavey's point of view, the Marconi system had been shown in service to be reasonably reliable and capable of working over ranges of sixty kilometres and more. The cross-Channel transmissions had demonstrated that radio telegraphy might eventually become either a useful supplement or else a dangerous rival to the Imperial network of submarine cables, and it was this aspect of policy which received the most attention in Post Office discussions. In contrast, the department's correspondence after January 1899 tended to disclaim any overriding responsibility to provide wireless communication with lighthouses and lightships. It was even stated that the Board of Trade had revived their old objections to the presence of apparatus which might distract keepers from their other duties.[27] Rather more convincingly, the Post Office solicitor had determined that the government's rights under the Patents, Designs and Trade Marks Act of 1883 did not cover the needs of Trinity House.[28] The Post Office could override an inventor's rights only when these obstructed vital government signals. They could not, in general, use radio communications without first being assured of the co-operation of the Wireless Telegraph and Signal Company.

The new Post Office policy was stated clearly in a memorandum forwarded to the Treasury in April 1899. Two crucial factors were identified; the probability of further technical improvements in the Marconi system, and the importance of protecting the nation's submarine cable interests. It was believed to be 'impossible to say how the situation may be affected by the further development of the invention; and it seems desirable, therefore, to act at once, in defence of the interests of the State'. Abandoning their earlier view that no aid should be given to private inventors for speculative research, the Post Office authorities now suggested that 'so remarkable an invention' should be investigated by their own engineers, 'even at some financial risk'. This would best be done by resuming co-operation with Marconi and his Company. With the approval of the Treasury, the Post Office therefore intended to negotiate for 'the right to use the invention for any purposes of the Crown and to settle the terms of a single agreement on behalf of the State'. There would then be no problem about granting a licence for the proposed ship-to-shore communications service, which the Post Office suggested, should be at a very moderate fee.[29]

This was a significant change, and a constructive one, in Post Office attitudes. It was left to Preece, from his less influential position as a private consultant, to suggest cynically that the Company should be left to enjoy what he called 'their imaginary strength', while the Post Office concentrated on developing the inductive system.[30] What cynicism of this kind remained within the Civil Service was principally the Treasury's prerogative. Still following their traditional policy of financial caution, they were not prepared to offer more to the Wireless Telegraph and Signal Company than was absolutely necessary. Treasury correspondence emphasised the pressures − the existence of the inductive telegraph, the government's rights under the Patents Acts, and the various counter-claims made against the Marconi patent − which might be brought to bear on the Company in any negotiations. It appears that Treasury officials believed the government to be in a strong bargaining position; they were not prepared to suggest any financial sum for the right to use Marconi's invention, as the grant of a licence, as requested, for ship-to-shore working was itself, they believed, adequate compensation.[31]

Evidently, the Treasury did not consider the Marconi system − despite the opinions of the Post Office and the Royal Navy − to be vital to the national interest, and their protracted discussions on the subject with other government departments occupied some six months. Eventually, in August 1899, they authorised the Post Office to negotiate with the Company on the government's behalf, but with very restricted terms of reference.[32] Gavey's engineering staff had abandoned Preece's claim that radio had been developed mainly as a result of Post Office support, and had indicated that they were prepared to accept a degree of risk in financing further research. These two concessions might have provided a useful basis for discussions, but the Treasury's parsimony left virtually no margin for negotiation.

The faults were not all on the government's side. Some scientists openly expressed their distrust of the Company's directors. Erskine Murray, working at the time as their Experimental Assistant, later described them as commercially-minded and as 'rather a shady lot'.[33] An editorial writer in *Nature* complained sourly of the Company's publicity campaign: 'The fact is that we have in these repeated sensational experiments a pure scientific apparatus boomed by energetic financial speculators for their own individual gain, and not for the benefit of the public − the worst feature of this money-grubbing age.'[34] The directors themselves might well have retorted that their attitudes were no more than were to be expected in a capitalist society from the representatives of investors who had not received a dividend after more than two years. In any case, they had provided more in the way of an offshore service 'for the benefit of the public' than the publicly-owned telegraphs could offer.

But Henry Allen, the Company's secretary, believed that the directors were not looking after their shareholders' interests: He complained that '... as long as the Board are undecided as to the price they put on their patents or the royalties to be charged for the use of the instruments then no business can be conducted with satisfaction to anyone working in this office be he Managing Director, Secretary, or otherwise engaged.'[35] This criticism was justified, at least in the early stages of the negotiations. The Company had asked for a licence for their proposed ship-to-shore service in December 1898, but it was more than three months before they decided that the service would be financed by a charge of about tenpence a word on each message. Allen's complaints were taken seriously, at least to the extent that the resumed negotiations with the Post Office in August 1899 concentrated on financial rather than technological prospects for radio telegraphy.

However, the Company's subsequent offer was quite incompatible with the Treasury's policy. The Treasury still believed that the grant of a licence for ship-to-shore working would, on its own, be enough to recompense the Company for any government use of its rights. But the Company suggested to the Post Office that they should be granted a free licence, as messages intended for inland addresses would be forwarded over the public telegraphs and so generate extra revenue for the Post Office. In addition, they offered to sell their patent rights for all government purposes (including the use of radio by the Army or the Royal Navy in any part of the world) in the United Kingdom for an annual payment of £30,000, or in all British Possessions for an annual payment of £50,000.[36] This offer was supported by a letter referring to the rise in price of the Company's shares as evidence of the commercial value of the patents.[37] The acountants at the Post Office, deduced, probably correctly, that the Company hoped to acquire a sinking fund which would replace their paid-up capital within the remaining term of validity of the original Marconi patent.[38]

The negotiators from the Post Office were in an impossible position so long as both the Company and the Treasury maintained their demands. As the price quoted by the Company was considerably in excess of what seemed reasonable (Preece had suggested an offer of £10,000 for the same rights in 1897), it was hoped that it would not be too difficult to get some reduction in the figure. But, despite considerable correspondence which pointed out that the rise in value of Marconi shares was not due to any experience of operating at a profit, and which stated plainly that the Post Office considered the price asked for the patent rights to be excessive, the Company's directors refused to modify their proposals. Accordingly, the Post Office negotiators advised the Company in October 1899 that 'this Department is not in a position to enter into any further negotiations'.[39]

And so hopes of co-operation between the Post Office and the Wireless Telegraph and Signal Company were, again, frustrated. The government's telegraph engineers in the Post Office service were to be employed mainly in attempts to reduce the influence of Marconi and his sponsors by testing radio apparatus from other suppliers. They consequently made little contribution to the technological development of radio during the rest of the nineteenth century. Technical experimentation continued within the Wireless Telegraph and Signal Company, but the failure to secure either government orders or a licence for independent working was a severe blow to the Company's hopes. Special demonstrations had been organised for the French and the United States' navies during 1899, but it was evident by the end of the year that there were not to be any profitable orders from these services. For the time being the Royal Navy was the only organisation with both an operational need for radio telegraphy and the technical resources to meet that need. But they were precluded, by Treasury instructions, from negotiating with the Wireless Telegraph and Signal Company.

References

1   Resolution of the Directors of the Wireless Telegraph and Signal Company Ltd, 19 August 1897 (PO, file E 23109/1899).

2   Post Office Solicitor to Secretary of the Post Office, 6 August 1897 (PO, file E 23109/1899).

3   Secretary of the Post Office to W. H. Preece, 9 August 1897 (PO, file E 23109/1899).

4   W. H. Preece to the Postmaster-General, 26 August 1897 (PO, file E 23109/1899).

5   D. Paresce-Marconi, *My Father Marconi*, Wimbledon, Muller, 1962, p. 54.

6   J. Gavey, 'Report by Engineer-in-Chief of the Post Office on the Technical Aspect of Wireless Telegraphy', 28 November 1902 (PO, file E 26411/03).

7   W. H. Preece, 'Report by the Engineer-in-Chief of the General Post Office on Recent Experiments with the so-called Wireless Telegraphy', 29 October 1897 (PRO, file ADM 116/523).

8 G. Marconi to W. H. Preece, 3 October 1897 (PO, file E 23109/1899).

9 Captain H. B. Jackson to C-in-C Devonport, 15 October 1897 (PRO, file ADM 116/523).

10 Gavey, 'Technical Aspect of Wireless Telegraphy'.

11 Secretary of the Post Office to the Wireless Telegraph and Signal Company, 22 October 1897 (PO, file ENG. 26173/1903).

12 *The Electrician*, XXXIX, 1897, pp. 865–8.

13 G. Marconi, 'Wireless Telegraphy', *Proc. Inst. Electr. Eng.*, XXVIII, 1899, pp. 290–1.

14 W. J. Baker, *A History of the Marconi Company*, London, Methuen, 1970, p. 38.

15 R. J. Chamberlain, 'Notes Compiled on the Occasion of the Coastal Radio Station Jubilee', October 1959 (Lloyd's Intelligence Department).

16 Marconi, *Wireless Telegraphy*, pp. 294–6.

17 Anon, ' "Spark telegraphy" in Germany', *The Electrician*, XL, 1897, p. 112.

18 British Patent Specification No. 11, 575 of 1897.

19 Marconi, *Wireless Telegraphy*, pp. 290–5.

20 Paresce-Marconi, *My Father Marconi*, pp. 72–6.

21 H. B. Jackson to G. Marconi, 29 May 1898 (MARCONI, file HIS 64).

22 Marconi, *Wireless Telegraphy*, p. 296.

23 *The Times*, 3 April 1899.

24 Wireless Telegraph and Signal Company to the Secretary of the Post Office, 12 September 1899 (PO, file ENG. 26173/1903).

25 Baker, *History of Marconi Company*, p. 49.

26 Secretary of the Post Office to the Wireless Telegraph and Signal Company, 9 August 1898 (PO, file ENG. 26173/1903).

27 Report of an Interview between J. C. Lamb and H. Jameson-Davis, 24 February 1899 (PO, file ENG. 26173/1903).

28 Post Office to Treasury, 22 June 1899 (PO, file ENG. 26173/1903).

29 Post Office to Treasury, 12 April 1899 (PO, file ENG. 26173/1903).

30 E. C. Baker, *Sir William Preece, FRS: Victorian Engineer Extraordinary*, London, Hutchinson, 1976, p. 279.

31 Treasury to Post Office, 9 May 1899 (PO, file ENG. 26173/1903).

32 Treasury to Post Office, 8 August 1899 (PO, file ENG. 26173/1903).

33 D. Wilson, *Rutherford, Simple Genius*, London, Hodder & Stoughton, 1983, p. 201.

34 *Nature*, LIX, 1899, p. 607.

35 W. P. Jolly, *Marconi*, London, Constable, 1972, p. 87.

36 Wireless Telegraph and Signal Company to Post Office, 1 September 1899, (PO, file ENG. 26173/1903).

37 Wireless Telegraph and Signal Company to Post Office, 12 September 1899 (PO, file ENG. 26173/1903).

38 Post Office to Wireless Telegraph and Signal Company, 6 September 1899 (PO, file ENG. 26173/1903).

39 Post Office to Wireless Telegraph and Signal Company, 5 October 1899 (PO, file ENG. 26173/1903).

12

A naval contract

... this system of wireless telegraphy is absolutely invaluable.
Vice-Admiral Sir Compton Domville, 1899

Following the failure of their negotiations with the Post Office, and perhaps reacting as well to the criticisms from their own Company Secretary, the directors of the Wireless Telegraph and Signal Company implemented a series of important changes in their organisation. These changes were marked by an alteration in the Company's name. Its new title, Marconi's Wireless Telegraph Company Ltd., adopted on 23 February 1900, was just as descriptive of the Company's activities and corresponded more closely with the already popular name of 'Marconi's'. (The name was changed again in 1963 to The Marconi Company Ltd.)

Jameson Davis resigned from his post as Managing Director in August 1899, and so his successor, Major Flood Page was responsible for the successful completion of most of the changes. With the unsatisfactory outcome, and consequent loss of expected business, after the prolonged negotiations with the Post Office, it was clearly necessary to reduce the Company's expenditure while seeking other sources of income. Flood Page began by closing the laboratories at the Haven Hotel, Poole and transferring all experimental work to the Company's factory at Chelmsford. As a further economy, Erskine Murray's full-time appointment in charge of the laboratories was abolished soon afterwards. As a less expensive alternative, a part-time scientific consultant was engaged instead in July 1900; Fleming, already acquainted with Marconi through his interest in the cross-Channel transmissions, accepted this post.

A commercial ship-to-shore service

Flood Page's main concern was to find new business. Reductions in personnel and other strict economies were all very well for a start but were not enough on their own to create a viable enterprise. It was essential to secure the orders which would generate a regular income, as opposed to the temporary, though often spectacular, individual contracts for such tasks as reporting sporting events which had provided most of the Company's trade. Since there was little prospect, for the time being, of getting orders from the Post Office, the directors re-considered the idea of starting their own private ship-to-shore telegraph service which had first been proposed in the autumn of 1898. Unfortunately, intervening events had effectively precluded the issue of the necessary licence to operate this service.

In fact, the Post Office themselves had identified a way out of this dilemma, though they had not mentioned their solution to the Company's negotiators. As early as August 1898, when the Company were first warned about the risks of infringing the Postmaster-General's telegraph monopoly, the Post Office's solicitor[1] had commented that there would have been no breach of the monopoly if both the transmitter and the receiver used at the Kingstown regatta had been owned and operated by the same party. While a public service financed from a charge on each individual message would be illegal, the regular exchange of signals between a ship's transmitter and a shore station which both belonged to the same company would be classed as a private telegraph line and consequently permitted within the law. The Company's solicitors[2] considered that such a service would be legal even when the owners of the radio apparatus operated the service on behalf of another party, provided that there were no charge for individual messages.[3] Marconi's radio link operated for Lloyds between Rathlin Island and Ballycastle would have been a good example of a legal private service of this kind.

While, however, the Company might reasonably expect to sell radio transmitters and receivers for shipowners to install in their own vessels, these same shipowners would not want to purchase the associated shore stations. Apart from the question of extra cost, there would be problems of interference between adjacent stations belonging to different owners. The obvious and preferable alternative was for Marconi's themselves to own the shore stations, and that would mean that they must own the ship-board installations as well. And so the organisation of the maritime communications business was defined to meet the legal requirements – the Marconi group owning the shore stations and the ships' sets, with the shipping companies hiring both the ships' radio apparatus *and its operators* from Marconi's. A subsidiary company, the Marconi International Marine Communication Company Ltd., was incorporated in April 1900 to handle this particular traffic. Its main offices were in Brussels, with offices and agencies in London, Paris and Rome to emphasise the Company's hope of securing international orders. The operating and manufacturing functions were thereby separated into two distinct groups at this very early stage in the radio industry's existence.

The Company had already received their first important order for ship-to-shore radio from a merchant shipping line. It was not from a British shipowner, but from one of their major German rivals, Norddeutscher Lloyd of Bremen. Three installations were involved, one for the liner *Kaiser Wilhelm der Grosse*, one for the Borkum Riff lightship, and one for the Borkum lighthouse which, by permission of the German government, was to be the shore station for the signalling link. These sets, again installed by the invaluable Kemp, went into operation when the liner sailed from Bremen on 28 February 1900.[4]

The Royal Navy's decision to adopt radio telegraphy

During all these negotiations with the British Post Office and with German shipping lines, the Company had also been careful to keep in touch with their most promising potential customer, the Royal Navy. Not wanting to miss any opportunity for demonstrating their latest apparatus in service conditions, the Company's directors offered to lend the sets needed for the Fleet's annual manoeuvres in 1899, charging only for the carriage of the equipment and the expenses of the technicians who would install and maintain it.[5]

This borrowed apparatus operated impeccably. The manoeuvres, which started on 27 July 1899, required the defending 'B' Fleet, with ten battleships and twenty cruisers, to rendezvous with an incoming convoy (represented by two cruisers) in the Atlantic and escort it safely to a British port. 'A' Fleet, with eight battleships and nineteen cruisers, was to attempt to intercept the convoy and prevent its safe arrival. Three vessels, all in 'B' Fleet, were fitted with Marconi radio sets – the battleship HMS *Alexandra*, flagship of Vice-Admiral Sir

Compton Domville, and two cruisers, HMS *Europa* and HMS *Juno*. This latter cruiser, manned mostly by reservists, was commanded by Jackson who had been recalled from Paris for the duration of the exercise. Its radio equipment was maintained by Marconi on his company's behalf.[6] If the radio in this ship had failed, it would not have been due to the lack of experienced radio engineers!

The manoeuvres began when Domville sent one squadron of cruisers, including HMS *Europa*, ahead of his battlefleet to locate the convoy as quickly as possible. A second cruiser squadron, led by HMS *Juno*, patrolled the flanks of his force, looking out for opposing vessels from 'A' Fleet. On reaching the rendezvous, the wireless operator in HMS *Europa* contacted his opposite number in HMS *Juno*, who in turn relayed the message to Domville's flagship: '*Juno* to Flag – Communicated with *Europa* about 60 miles off convoy rendezvous. She was there with convoy, and has now returned to squadron. Convoy following at about nine knots. No enemy sighted by her or by us'.[7] This signal was transmitted to the Admiral over more than 150 kilometres – the greatest range which had been achieved at that time by any marine signalling system using only one relaying vessel.

'B' Fleet escorted the convoy into Milford Haven on 3 August, and were accordingly declared to be the victors. 'A' Fleet's scouts had not sighted the convoy during the exercise, though cruisers from the opposing forces were in contact briefly at the very end of the manoeuvres.

Domville's success was due in part to the intelligent use of radio by his Fleet, but even more to the total absence of radio in his rival's command. When 'A' Fleet's patrols first located the main force of 'B' Fleet, it had taken fifty-five hours for this vital intelligence to reach their commander – far too long an interval for him to make use of the information.[8] The overall results were all that the advocates of radio within the Royal Navy could have hoped. Domville himself was in no doubt as to the utility of wireless communication, reporting officially that

from my own experience of its use during the past month, I consider from the Admiral's point of view, that this system of wireless telegraphy is absolutely invaluable. It can be trusted, especially at night or in a fog, when no other system is perfectly reliable. I would submit that the proposals to fit certain ships with it be carried into effect as soon as possible.[9]

Domville had discovered in practice that radio could solve one of the Fleet's communications problems — it enabled an Admiral to keep in touch with the scattered units under his command. But the manoeuvres had also shown that radio could help to increase the effective radius of operation of a cruiser squadron escorting a convoy. The new technology might well prove to be a useful contribution towards solving the even greater problem of providing adequate protection for the Empire's merchant shipping.

The suggestion to fit some warships with Marconi sets was endorsed enthusiastically by the interested officers at the Board of Admiralty. Rear Admiral Archibald Douglas, then Second Naval Lord[10] with special responsibility for the Royal Navy's personnel, proposed the immediate purchase of eight Marconi sets for familiarisation and training of signalmen in the Channel and Mediterranean squadrons.[11] Rear Admiral A.K. Wilson, the Third Naval Lord — who was responsible for the Fleet's equipment — advised that radio was essential for the fighting efficiency of the Royal Navy, and suggested that it would not be wise to postpone ordering the necessary sets until after the conclusions of negotiations between the Post Office and the Wireless Telegraph and Signal Company.[12] But, even before this suggestion could be considered, the Post Office warned that they did not expect to reach an agreement.[13] George Goschen, First Lord of the Admiralty, carefully reassessed his Department's position before authorising the acquisition of radio sets for the Fleet. He decided that the Wireless Telegraph and Signal Company should be told that, the negotiations having failed, the Admiralty considered themselves free to procure such apparatus as they needed under the terms of the Patents, Designs and Trade Marks Act of 1883. When the Treasury and the General Post Office had also been told of this decision, then, Goschen said, he would approve an order for the eight radio sets which Douglas had requested.[14]

Accordingly, on 7 December 1899, a letter was sent to the Company, thanking them for the 'loan of instruments for use during the recent Manoeuvres', but at the same time regretting that as the negotiations with the Post Office had been broken off, the Admiralty's '... only course is to proceed to set up installations on their own account, and to manufacture the articles in question, under the powers reserved to the Crown by section 27 of the "Patents, Designs, and Trade Marks Act, 1883", viz: "To use the invention for the service of the Crown, on such terms as may be settled by the Treasury after hearing all parties interested.'"[15] This particular legal clause had first been identified by the Post Office's solicitor in 1897 as a possible method of bringing pressure on the Company to concede patent rights which were not then thought to be of very great interest to the government. Now, however, it was being invoked as, apparently, the only means of acquiring apparatus needed urgently by a government department.

Letters were sent to the Treasury and to the Post Office telling them of this decision. These other departments were not informed of another, more conciliatory message which had been sent from the Admiralty to the Company, assuring them that the Royal Navy would 'be glad to give full consideration to any proposals which you may be able to make for granting the use of your patents on more reasonable terms, observing that any arrangements made with the Admiralty alone would have to be framed as not to commit other departments of Her Majesty's Government'.[16] By the end of 1899, the need for radio telegraphy was regarded as so urgent that no means of acquiring the best apparatus was to be neglected. Evidently, though, the Royal Navy's officers doubted whether other branches of the government service shared their opinion.

The adoption of radio by the Royal Navy

Jackson would have approved of these attempts to maintain good relations with the Wireless Telegraph and Signal Company. He had been recalled from the Paris embassy in the autumn of 1899 for temporary attachment to HMS *Vernon*, the torpedo school at Portsmouth. His duties there were defined as 'imparting to the officers of the torpedo branch the results of the experience gained by him during several years of experiments ... working out the many small details required for ship fittings of the Marconi apparatus ... establishing a course of instruction for the operators'.[17] Within a few weeks, when it became obvious that the expected Marconi apparatus would not be available for some time, Jackson's duties were expanded to include supervision of the design and construction of the naval sets to be made under the provisions of the Patents Act. Nevertheless, his first report from this new appointment recommended that the Royal Navy should be careful to keep on good terms with the Company so that they would be 'posted up in all the latest improvements' to the Marconi system.[18]

He also reported that he was designing the Royal Navy's sets to resemble the Marconi system as closely as possible. When, as Jackson hoped, Marconi sets became available, signalmen would be able to transfer from one system to the other with little or no cross-training. In addition, there would be no need to provision separate spare parts for the two different systems. But, despite this similarity in design, he admitted that these sets were not reaching the same standards of performance as those designed and built by Marconi. These early indications were confirmed as the sets were brought into service during the early months of 1900, their maximum range being about fifty kilometres at the best (as against sixty-five kilometres or more for Marconi apparatus). The annual manoeuvres of the Fleet, from 24 July to 3 August 1900, were a severe disappointment to those who recalled the spectacular success of the Marconi radio equipment in the previous year's exercises. Four of the *Vernon* sets were issued to each fleet for the manoeuvres; those in 'A' Fleet were reported as working well, but unable to achieve ranges better than thirty kilometres, while those in 'B' Fleet failed completely because of poor insulation.[19] The only encouraging feature of the manoeuvres was the high standard of working in those ships where the apparatus were operating satisfactorily, which was considered to reflect the quality of training in the *Vernon* and *Defiance* establishments.

Fortunately, the Royal Navy kept in touch with the Marconi company. A week after receiving the Admiralty's letter offering to consider any reasonable terms which the Company might propose, Flood Page visited the Admiralty for an interview with Rear Admiral Wilson. The latter reported that Flood Page had assured him the Company did not consider the letters from the Admiralty as being in any sense hostile (after all, it was obviously in the Company's interest to cultivate its connections with the one government department which had admitted to a need for radio telegraphy). Understanding the Admiralty's difficulties, Flood Page had offered to lend the eight sets which Douglas wanted on the same terms as the three sets loaned for the 1899 manoeuvres.[20]

As the relatively poor performance of the Royal Navy's own radio apparatus was already becoming evident, the Board of Admiralty were grateful for this offer. It could not, however, be accepted immediately; there first had to be discussion with other government departments and particularly with the General Post Office. In this exchange of letters, the Admiralty were careful to emphasise the 'extreme importance' of the Marconi system to the Fleet, and the lack of any other wireless telegraphy system with comparable performance.

The discussion delayed any decision until March 1900. Flood Page then abruptly withdrew his previous offer to lend eight sets. Claiming that the Company would be unable to spare the services of two assistants at that time, he also pointed out that 'we are a Company existing among other things for commercial purposes and it seems to us most unbusinesslike that no decisions should be arrived at as to the amount which HM Government should pay to this Company for the use of the Marconi system on board the Ships of the Navy'.[21] But the discussions between the various government departments concerned had progressed so far that it was no longer necessary to arrange for the loan of apparatus. The Post Office had already acknowledged the importance of equipping the Royal Navy's ships as quickly as possible and regretted being themselves unable to supply apparatus as efficient as the Marconi system. In the circumstances, they had no objection to a separate agreement between the Admiralty and the Company, but suggested that any such agreement should be for a limited number of sets.

In fact, there was no reason for objection from the Post Office. Radio sets fitted in the Royal Navy's warships would not infringe the Postmaster General's telegraph monopoly. With the Post Office having agreed, the Treasury, too, said that they had no objection to separate arrangements between the Admiralty and Marconi's company for a limited number of sets at an annual royalty of £100 for each installation (the amount suggested by the Company's directors after their initial discussions with the Admiralty early in 1899).[22] Having secured the Treasury's permission, the Admiralty sent a letter of intent to the Company, asking for thirty-two sets of apparatus.[23] Delivery of these sets from the Chelmsford factory started in September 1900, the entire order being completed by the end of November. A contract formalising the order and confirming the price of each complete installation to be £196 14s 4d, plus a royalty of £100 a year, was signed by both parties on 20 February 1901. An additional clause, inserted at the request of the Post Office, stipulated that payment of the royalty did not constitute an admission of the validity of the Marconi patents.

It was not an exaggeration when the Royal Navy's officers claimed that they had an urgent need for these sets. The world-wide commitments of the Fleet had increased considerably during 1899 and 1900, with fears of a European war after the Fashoda incident, followed by the outbreak of hostilities in South Africa and threats against British residents in China during the Boxer rising. Four Marconi sets, acquired from the Army in South Africa, were installed in cruisers blockading the neutral port of Laurenco Marques to intercept supplies intended for the Transvaal. Threee of the *Vernon* sets were shipped to the China Squadron, where they were used to co-ordinate operations between shore parties and ships at sea. The new sets delivered from Marconi's were immediately sent to ships and shore establishments throughout the Empire, as detailed in Table 12.1.[24]

While this apparatus was being brought into service, a further fifty-two sets were ordered from the workshops of HMS *Vernon*. These were of a new design, with performance comparable to the latest Marconi equipment. The original *Vernon* sets were gradually withdrawn and modified to bring them up to these new standards.

Table 12.1   *Allocations of Marconi sets as at 31 December 1900*

Channel Squadron	6
Mediterranean Squadron	4
China Squadron	3
Reserve Squadron	3
Training Squadron	4
Torpedo schools	4
Shore stations	8

Source: HMS *Vernon* Annual Report, 1900, p. 125.

Experience with the radio sets in service had confirmed that they did, indeed, enable an Admiral to keep in contact with distant vessels in his fleet. More important, this experience, and particularly during the 1899 manoeuvres and in the South African blockade, had also shown that cruisers could operate independently over large areas of the sea, co-ordinating their operations effectively, provided that they were fitted with radio. There was, at last, a chance of providing proper protection for the Empire's trade routes.

Discussions of possible strategies were re-opened in 1899 after the Fashoda incident. Eventually, a meeting was called at the Admiralty in April 1905 to formulate the first truly comprehensive plan to protect merchant shipping. This was based on cruiser squadrons stationed at vital places where several trade routes converged; chains of radio-equipped patrol vessels along the trade routes would keep in contact with the responsible Admirals and advise them immediately of the presence of enemy raiders.[25]

The expansion of marine radio facilities in the early twentieth century also solved one other outstanding problem of nineteenth-century maritime communications: the provision of an offshore telegraph for emergency signals. Although the Post Office had made little progress towards their perceived task of providing such a method of communicating between light vessels and the shore, the need for this kind of wireless telegraph became less urgent after the foundation of the Marconi International Marine Company. A Marconi shore terminal could handle emergency messages as well as commercial traffic; a merchant ship in distress could itself call for help, provided it were fitted with a radio transmitter. In August 1902, in spite of the opposition of the Post Office, a notice was inserted in the *London Gazette* by the Hydrographic Department of the Admiralty, advising merchant shipping of the locations of Marconi shore stations. This was undoubtedly useful publicity for the new communications service, presenting its work in humanitarian as well as commercial terms. The offshore telegraph – and the Company which provided it – had been aided considerably by the co-operation of the Royal Navy.

Marconi's company is a good example of the sort of business which has more recently been identified by Ghemawat as progressing by 'improvement in general technical knowledge and inputs plus feedback from customers', and in which, according to Ghemawat, the correct marketing strategy is 'to maximise bargaining power with suppliers and buyers'.[26] In a labour-intensive industry with little specialised plant – such as the radio industry in its early years – the suppliers of materials are less influential than the customers' buyers, at least while output remains relatively low. Ghemawat's analysis therefore suggests that the Company adopted the correct policy, trying to cultivate its contacts within the Post Office and the Royal Navy, while using the information it received from the Royal Navy as feedback to improve its product so as to meet the customers' needs. This policy was seen to work well, in that the Company secured exclusive rights to supply the world's largest market, the Royal Navy, for marine communications equipment, and was eventually able to compete successfully with the more modern Telefunken organisation. This policy was effectively recognised at the time by the Company's directors, Flood Page writing to *The Times* in July 1900 about the importance of the naval contract to the Company's survival.[27]

With each set coasting just under two hundred pounds, and an annual royalty on each set of one hundred pounds, the whole of the 1900 order (thirty-two sets) brought in a capital sum of about £6,000 and a further income of £3,200 a year for the following decade. By the standards of the late nineteenth century, this was a fairly substantial amount of money for a business which still relied on hand-craftsmanship in conditions resembling a hobbyist's workshop. It was less than the optimistic £30,000 which Jameson Davis had asked in the 1899 negotiations – but the total received in the first year of the contract was little short of the £10,000 which Preece had suggested in 1897 was a reasonable price for the outright purchase of Marconi's patent rights. Moreover, the Company had in addition secured a guaranteed annual income, and had not surrendered any of their rights in return. This was a good financial basis, not only for the Company's survival, but for the expansion of its business in the twentieth century.

References

1   Post Office Solicitor to Secretary of the Post Office, 9 August 1898 (PO, file E 23109/1899).

2   W. J. Baker, *A History of the Marconi Company*, London, Methuen, 1970, pp. 58–60.

3   Although the formal records imply that the Company's solicitors arrived independently at the same conclusion, it is, of course, possible that this information was passed unofficially to the Company by a sympathetic civil servant.

4   Baker, *Marconi Company*, pp. 57–8; H. Goetzeler, 'Ferdinand Braun und die Drahtlosen Telegraphia an der Nordsee', *Deutsches Schiffahrtsarchiv*, V, 1975, pp. 151–8.

5   Wireless Telegraph and Signal Company Ltd to Director of Navy Contracts, 3 July 1898 (PRO, file ADM 116/567).

6   Captain H. B. Jackson to Vice-Admiral Sir Compton Domville, 25 July 1899 (PRO, file ADM 116/523).

7   *The Times*, 4 August 1899.

8   R. F. Pocock and G. R. M. Garratt, *The Origins of Maritime Radio*, London, The Science Museum, 1972, p. 30.

9   Remarks by Vice-Admiral Sir Compton Domville, 11 August 1899 (PRO, file ADM 116/523).

10   Senior officers on the Board of Admiralty at this time were known as Naval Lords, instead of the traditional title of Sea Lords as used both before and since the late nineteenth century.

11 Minute of Second Naval Lord, 17 August 1899 (PRO, file ADM 116/567).

12 Minute of A. K. Wilson, 21 August 1899 (PRO, file ADM 116/567).

13 General Post Office to Admiralty, 6 September 1899 (PRO, file ADM 116/567).

14 Minute of First Lord of the Admiralty, 8 November 1899 (PRO, file ADM 116/567).

15 Admiralty to Wireless Telegraph and Signal Company, 7 December 1899 (PRO, file ADM 116/523).

16 *Ibid.*

17 Admiralty to C-in-C, Portsmouth, 26 October 1899 (PRO, file ADM 116/523).

18 Minute of Captain H. B. Jackson, 10 November 1899 (PRO, file ADM 116/567).

19 'Annual Report of the Torpedo School (HMS *Vernon*)' for 1900, pp. 95–102 (NHL).

20 Report of Meeting between Major Flood Page and Rear Admiral A. K. Wilson, 14 December 1899 (PRO, file ADM 116/567).

21 Marconi's Wireless Telegraph Company Ltd to Admiralty, 26 March 1900 (PRO, file ADM 116/567).

22 Treasury to Admiralty, 5 April 1900 (PRO, file ADM 116/567).

23 Admiralty to Marconi's Wireless Telegraph Company Ltd, 8 May 1900 (PRO, file ADM 116/567).

24 HMS *Vernon* Annual Report, 1900, pp. 108–10, 125 (NHL).

25 ' A. J. Marder, *The Anatomy of British Sea Power: a History of British Naval Policy in the Pre-Dreadnought Era, 1880–1905*, London, Frank Cass & Co., 1964, pp. 98–102.

26 P. Ghemawat, 'Building strategy on the experience curve', *Harvard Business Review*, LXIV, 1985, p. 145.

27 *The Times*, 18 July 1900.

Conclusion

The State as a commercial sponsor

The radio equipment supplied to the Royal Navy under the 1900 contract developed from the apparatus which Hertz had used for his researches in 1887. When these researches were discussed by the British Association at their Bath meeting, Lodge remarked prophetically that '... the now recognised fact that light is an electric oscillation must have before long a profound practical import'.[1] It is now evident that this prophecy was to be fulfilled in rather less than ten years. With the benefit of hindsight it is possible to trace a rapid and apparently logical progression from the laboratory experiments to a useful means of maritime communication. But when Lodge made his prediction, it was by no means obvious that he was, in fact, forecasting a system of marine wireless telegraphy.

Recognition of a need for a marine communications system

Even those applied scientists who were themselves investigating the properties of this newly-discovered electromagnetic radiation would not necessarily have foreseen the outcome of their work as early as the 1880s. When Lodge made his prophecy to the British Association, he continued by describing his own observations of electromagnetic waves on lightning conductors. Anyone who was then among his audience might well have expected to see this knowledge first put to use in some new branch of meteorology. This expectation would not have been disabused by later published work from Fitzgerald and Tesla in 1892 and 1893, discussing the properties of terrestrial and atmospheric electromagnetic radiation, by Thomson's observations of the effects of lightning discharges on electro-plating baths in 1894, or by the construction and description of Popov's thunderstorm detector in 1895.

It was not until three years after Lodge's prophecy that Trotter's editorial article in *The Electrician* first suggested using the newly – discovered Hertzian waves for maritime signalling. In the following year, Crookes wrote in the *Fortnightly Review* about the properties of a wireless telegraph such as Trotter had suggested. Although Crookes did not propose this telegraph specifically for use at sea, he did emphasise that its performance would not be impaired by fog, then recognised as one of a mariner's greatest worries. Tesla was rather more precise; writing in the *Journal of the Franklin Institute* in 1893, he recommended that his proposed wireless telegraph should first be tested in a ship at sea. Somewhat more obliquely, even Preece contributed to this idea of a new method of marine telegraphy by comparing his own inductive wireless telegraph system with a light-house during his presentation to the British Association in 1894 (though he was mistaken when he implied that his apparatus utilised Hertzian waves). By late 1895, both Popov in Russia and Jackson in Britain were experimenting with replicas of Hertz's and Lodge's laboratory apparatus in the course of their regular naval duties.

So far as British technical literature was concerned, the association of Hertzian-wave research with the idea of improved maritime communications started in about 1891 and developed over the next four years. This was also the time when the press campaign which Fisher and Stead had initiated in the *Pall Mall Gazette* was taken up as well by the *Fortnightly Review* and reached its successful culmination with the large increase in the Navy Estimates for 1893. The campaign for a larger and more powerful Fleet was paralleled by the Royal National Lifeboat Institution's sustained campaign for better coastal telegraphy, and particularly by Tyndall's writings in the *Fortnightly Review* and by frequent letters and editorial articles in *The Times*. It was, in fact, the problem of offshore rescue which had prompted Trotter's influential article in *The Electrician*. Evidently, the discussion of maritime signalling problems in the technical and scientific press was one consequence of the general increase of public interest in the Royal Navy and the merchant fleet which these political pressure-groups had initiated so skilfully.

The 'maritime myth' of the late nineteenth century affected scientific writers just as it was apparent in more popular branches of literature and music. Indeed, the language of Imperialism permeated the very words in which applied scientists described their achievements. Images of discovery, exploration, battle and military conquest abound in English-language scientific literature of the period. Maxwell's electromagnetic theory was described by Fitzgerald as 'cumbered with the debris of his entrenched camps, of his battles', while Heaviside had, according to Fitzgerald, 'opened up a direct route, ... made a broad road, and ... explored a considerable tract of country'.[3] Crookes was said by one of his friends to be 'a keen fighter, but the enemies he preferred to fight were the enemies of the human race. Thus he enlisted in the ranks against cattle plague and cholera when these pests were raging in England, and rapidly gained the higher command by his industry and keen insight.'[3] Tesla likewise considered the aim of science to be the subjugation of nature, claiming that 'to create and to annihilate material substance, cause it to aggregate in forms according to his desire, would be the supreme manifestation of the power of Man's mind his most complete triumph over the physical world, his crowning achievement.[4]

Lodge, friend and correspondent of both Crookes and Tesla, expressed the same idea of conquest in somewhat less dramatic terms by suggesting that 'Matter has many imperfections, and it is part of our business on this planet to struggle with it and coerce it to do what we want.'[5] Even the Italian-born Marconi was sufficiently influenced by Imperialist termonology as to declare that with the development of radio.

mankind not only has available a new and powerful means of scientific research, but it is conquering a new force and utilising a new arm of civilization and progress which knows no frontiers, and can even push out into infinite spaces where never before has the feeling of any manifestation of the activity and thought of man been able to penetrate.[6]

When (in the words quoted in the introduction to this study) Fitzgerald described Hertz's researches as a victory in 'the battle lost by the giants of old', he could be confident that a nineteenth-century audience of scientists would understand his reference to classical mythology. But it is as interesting now, that he should have chosen to evaluate a major scientific discovery in terms of the more modern mythology of Imperial conquest.

But those British applied scientists who contributed most to the development of radio were not merely influenced in their language by Imperialism and 'maritime myths'. They were active supporters of Fisher's political campaign. Heaviside, a recluse, spoke approvingly to his friends of Fisher's policy and methods.[7] Lodge, active in public life as physicist, educationalist and advocate of social reform, supported the increase in the 1893 Navy Estimates during an address to the British Association.[8] Jackson, a naval officer, was personally selected by Fisher a few years later to assist in the implementation of his naval reforms. Crookes, like Trotter, had worked as a consultant for the armed services. He chose to publish his ideas about wireless telegraphy in the *Fortnightly Review*, a journal already associated with the naval and offshore safety campaigns. Some years later, he would be a colleague of Fisher on the Admiralty's Inventions Board.

Applied science, socialism and national defence

None of these applied scientists, however, was employed as a telegraph engineer during the years from 1888 to 1896, when radio was developed from pure physics into a useful means of communication. Few of the country's telegraph engineers foresaw this development or appreciated its import. While memories of the financial scandals preceding Scudamore's resignation were reinforced regularly by the Post Office telegraph service's chronic operating deficit no one — and, least of all, those like Preece in posts of high responsibility within the Post Office — would risk investment in a new technology with no guarantee of a prompt return. This attitude would, by itself, have been quite correct for a government department charged with the disposal of public funds. Unfortunately, it was exacerbated by an excessive conservatism in technology, which itself was a symptom of a strong family tradition dating back to the early nineteenth century, before the existence of the nationalised telegraph service. Wheatstone had been a founder of the Electric Telegraph Company in 1845; Edwin and Latimer Clark had each in turn been the Company's Chief Engineer. In 1892, nearly half-a-century later, the Clarks' brother-in-law, William Preece, was the Post Office's Engineer-in-Chief, while Wheatstone's nephew, Arthur Heaviside, was one of Preece's principal assistants. Even at that late date, most of the senior engineers in the Post Office service had started their careers with the Electric Telegraph Company. When financial rectitude was combined with such a close-knit community spirit, there was little chance for an outsider to get a new idea accepted. Neither Bell's telephone nor Marconi's radio telegraph was regarded by the Post Office staff as anything more than a minor adjunct to the existing telegraph system. As a result, the telephone industry did not develop in Britain to the same extent that it did in Germany and the USA. This was the common experience of many high-technology industries of the period.

The radio industry was an exception. It was founded by a group of applied scientists who were *not* telegraph engineers.[9] Had some responsible body, such as the government or the Institution of Electrical Engineers, convened a committee of recognised communications experts to pronounce on the value of radio telegraphy at any time between 1895 and 1898, it would almost certainly have endorsed the Post Office's opinion that there was little merit in the new technology.

The engineering backgrounds of those individuals identified in this study as making the greatest contributions to the invention of radio are revealing, for they were from the mainstream of neither engineering nor of pure science. Hertz was a mechanical engineer working as a researcher in pure physics. Lodge was a self-educated academic; his friend Crookes was a scientific journalist who had also researched in pure physics and chemistry. Tesla was a consultant, chiefly known for his contributions to electrical power generation and distribution. Jackson was a torpedo expert. Heaviside and Marconi were amateurs living on private incomes. They were conscious of being regarded as 'outsiders' in the communities of engineers and mathematical physicists, and this common knowledge – whether real or imagined – helped to integrate them into a coherent group linked by mutual friendships and correspondence.

They were also linked by a common enthusiasm for social reform. In this respect, too, they differed from the established telegraph engineers, finding themselves more in sympathy with the electrical power engineers – like Sebastian de Ferranti – of whom Hennessey observes that

Typically, not a few of these electricians were Fabian-type socialists ... optimism and boyish confidence ... abounded ... in conflict with vested interests, their crusade was marked with great moral fervour ... it is significant that so many of these engineers did speculate about the future, for that is the manner of revolutionaries who imagine that they are 'on the side of the future'.[10]

The application of electrical science to industry became a moral crusade for these applied scientists. Electric lighting, which created no fumes and did not consume oxygen, had already contributed to a reduction in respiratory illness among office workers. A more wide-spread utilisation of electricity would eliminate much of the pollution associated with earlier power sources. As Lodge said, it would. '... restore our large towns to their old habitable beauty and healthfulness before the smoke-demon destroyed the vegetation and blackened the sky'.[11] The creation of a more 'green and pleasant' land would, the applied scientists claimed, improve health and elevate the moral outlook of workers. Their vision may well have been influenced by the 'rural myth' of British (and more specifically, of English) society which Wiener has identified. But their socialism was not the socialism of William Morris and the Arts and Craft Movement. While Morris and his colleagues looked back to an idealised form of medieval industry based on small self-contained rural workshops, Lodge and the applied scientists envisaged a post-industrial society in which cheap electrical power supplied by an integrated grid from large central generating stations (such as the systems which Tesla had designed) would mean that there would be little difference in living standards between town and country.

Professing a collectivist socialism controlled and supplied by a centralised authority, these applied scientists approved of such Unionist policies as the State control of education, the provision of State finance for scientific training and the maintenance of a State-owned telegraph system. They criticised these policies when progress did not seem sufficiently rapid, and they strongly opposed government measures which discouraged collectivisation, such as those Acts preventing the growth of monopolies in the tramway and electrical supply industries.

In practice, the main immediate result of these applied scientists' activities was the invention of an improved system of maritime communications for the Royal Navy, and so a strengthening of national defences in Britain and in her naval ally, Italy. This was quite consistent with contemporary socialist thought. Radical liberal politicians like Dilke, Hardie of the Independent Labour Party, and Hyndman of the Social Democratic Federation, all supported the political moves for the Royal Navy's expansion in the late nineteenth century.[12]

Social reformers had, in fact, been advocating the application of science to military purposes for more than a century. Writing during the eighteenth-century Industrial Revolution, Gibbon had claimed in his *Decline and Fall of the Roman Empire* that '... Cannon and fortifications now form an impregnable barrier ... Europe is secure from any future irruption of barbarians; since, before they can conquer, they must cease to be barbarous'. This identification of scholarship with military strength was also the theme of an address by Ruskin — socialist philosopher, and a correspondent of Lodge's — to young Army officers in 1865. Ruskin suggested, indeed, that the artistic achievements of ancient Greece and of the European Renaissance might somehow be essentially related to the military virtues of the armoured hoplites and knights whose prowess was celebrated in the literature of those eras.[13] By the late nineteenth century, the publication of Darwin's studies and other evolutionary writings was claimed to have provided a scientific justification for these opinions which could legitimately be extrapolated from biology to sociology. This kind of State-Darwinism appears many times in the works of the Fabian author H. G. Wells (1866–1946), who was another of Lodge's correspondents. In *The War of the Worlds*, published in 1898, Wells devotes the whole of the novel to the theme that war may be a force of natural selection, favouring more advanced civilisations at the expense of lesser beings. But it was after the traumatic shock of Britain's military reverses in the early stages of the Boer War that he produced his most explicit description of war as a Darwinist mechanism enabling the superior social order (which was, of course, Fabian state-socialism exploiting the full potential of applied science in Wells' opinion) to supplant more primitive human communities within the confines of this planet. Wells' hero in *The Land Ironclads*, says that

If a decent civilisation ... cannot produce better men for war than ... open-air life ... then civilisation has to stop ... the idea that any people living in the open air, hunting perpetually, losing touch with books and art and all the things that intensify life, might hope to resist and break that great development to the end of time, jarred on his civilised soul.

Eventually, in this novel, the more civilised army is victorious, using its applied science to defeat physically-superior enemies with machines that anticipate modern tanks.

It is interesting to note in the present context that Wells describes the successful commander as having the 'type of feature and expression that prevails in His Majesty's Navy: alert, intelligent, quiet'. This kind of idealisation of the maritime technician is also used in Wells' sociological novel *Tono-Bungay*. The failings of Britain's class-conscious, capitalist community are there depicted as they appear to a naval architect, and the novel closes when the narrator symbolically renounces that community by heading out to sea in his newest, fastest warship. By the early twentieth century, the 'maritime myth' was influencing Wells' socialist writings, just as it had influenced technical literature a decade earlier.

The acceptance of radio telegraphy by the Royal Navy

While, however, this 'maritime myth' had no doubt inspired the applied scientists' electromagnetic-wave research and so had encouraged the development of radio telegraphy, there was another important group of people involved in this development. The new method of communication had to be accepted by the officers of the Royal Navy before it could be installed in the nation's warships. And these professional naval officers might be expected to be less sentimental and more realistic than their civilian counterparts were about maritime affairs. Their backgrounds might suggest that they would have been even less receptive than the Post Office's engineers to new ideas. Potential naval officers were nominated for the service by existing officers; cadetships were then awarded to those candidates successful in a competitive examination. They received an extremely specialised education, very different from that of their contemporaries in the public schools. After commissioning, their professional lives were spent mostly at sea, remote from ordinary social contacts. Regarding themselves as an elite group, they were a close-knit community with traditions alien to most outsiders. It would probably have been more difficult to get a stranger's ideas accepted by the Royal Navy than by the Post Office in most circumstances. But when Marconi brought his radio telegraph to Britain, it was adopted by the Royal Navy and rejected by the Post Office telegraph service.

The important difference was that the Royal Navy had themselves recognised the need for a wireless telegraph, even before Marconi started development of his system. In contrast, the Post Office engineers had identified no such need in the course of their own routine duties. Problems in offshore communications had first been appreciated by the coastal rescue services, and it had been their skilful political lobbying which eventually imposed the task of developing a suitable wireless telegraph on to the Post Office. Naval officers, however, had themselves discovered the need for wireless telegraphy during their own torpedo-boat trials, and the instruction to develop a suitable system came from the flag officers, such as Tryon, who were already the acknowledged leaders of their elitist group. They were well-trained applied scientists, and could appreciate Marconi's achievement the better for having no tradition of conventional communications engineering to inhibit their judgment. Jackson's career was directed to the eventual command of a fleet and the many skills thereby entailed, not to the more specialised duties of an electrical engineer. He regarded Marconi as a colleague and not as a rival in his attempt to solve the communications problem, and Marconi's eventual success reflected some credit on Jackson.

Historically it was necessary for radio to be introduced successfully into the Royal Navy before the more cautious civil servants could be persuaded of its value. White and Graham have made a detailed study of the characteristics of such successful technological innovations in a capitalist economy.[14] They have identified four important factors, which, they claim, any new device must possess if it is to make a significant impact on existing methods. It must have inventive merit − the problems created by its introduction must be less than the problems which it is intended to solve; it must have embodiment merit − its introduction must provide scope for further improvements in other areas; it must have operational merit − existing working practices must be modified readily to take advantage of the new techniques; it must have market merit − it must open up sales opportunities which did not exist before, rather than just offering replacement of an earlier product. While some civil service departments could not recognise even the 'inventive merit' of radio − the Board of Trade for instance, claiming as late as 1899 that the operation of radio alarms would distract lighthouse keepers from more important duties − the Royal Navy already had the trained signalmen and technicians needed to operate and maintain radio sets. Once this 'inventive merit' had been recognised, and radio equipment had been tested by the Royal Navy, the 'embodiment merit' and 'operational merit' were evident. It was at last possible to take advantage of the various improvements in warship design over the previous twenty years, such as the higher speeds and greater ranges of guns which increased a cruiser's radius of action, without losing control of the more widely dispersed units under an Admiral's command. Existing practices of centralised, hierarchical control were strengthened by the introduction of this new method of communication. The way in which naval thinking had adapted so rapidly to incorporate experience with radio in service is illustrated by the allocations of thirty of the original Marconi sets; by 1901, eight of these sets were fitted in battleships, ten were in cruisers, eight were in shore stations, and only four were allocated to the torpedo schools and depot ships which had provided the initial impetus for the invention.[15]

Radio may also be said to have possessed very real 'market merit', so far as Marconi's company were concerned. Those sets which were sold to the Royal Navy and to the merchant service were intended for ship-to-ship and ship-to-shore communications which could not be provided by any other telegraph system. The new technology supplemented existing land lines and submarine cables, at least during the nineteenth and early-twentieth centuries, so that the Post Office were excessively cautious when regarding Marconi's invention as a rival to their own inductive telegraph and, later, to the cable network. But for the first few years of the industry's existence there was little need for a formal marketing strategy; the largest Fleet in the world would provide enough orders to absorb the output of most of the Company's manufacturing capacity. Any commercial orders secured through Marconi's tireless publicity would be in the nature of a bonus to the Company's regular income. The return from the Royal Navy involved more than money. Radio equipment loaned or sold to the Fleet, whether for experiment or routine use, in effect underwent extensive trials. It was operated and maintained by the Royal Navy's skilled technicians, and their observations were fed back to the Company. Engineers from the Company itself were sometimes (as during the 1899 manoeuvres) permitted to monitor the performance of the equipment in service. The officers of the Royal Navy thereby ensured that the main lines of radio development were directed towards meeting their own needs, but they also were effectively providing a generous subsidy meeting virtually all Marconi's research and development costs. This was in noticeable contrast to the contemporary experience of the German industry, whose products were not accepted by Tirpitz for the Imperial Fleet until they were demonstrably reliable in all conditions, and who consequently got no useful feedback from this important customer.[16]

The relationship of advanced technology to the State

This kind of government involvement in a new technology was a relatively new experience in Britain at the time. It was then unusual for a State department to co-operate with a commercial company so closely as the Royal Navy co-operated with the Marconi organisation.

Further nationalisations, and the extensive use of advanced technology by the armed services in two World Wars, have provided much more experience of such relationships. Seventy years after the foundation of the Wireless Telegraph and Signal Company, the criteria defined by Rowan as essential for successful government intervention in industry were:

(a) Industry must not accept that something is in the public interest merely because a Minister says so, unless he is announcing a policy approved by Parliament.

(b) We need to regard with greatest suspicion both requests for 'voluntary co-operation' and also the transfer of powers to parastatal bodies with roles not clearly defined and limited by Parliament.

(c) We must be careful not to be caught in the inconsistency of regarding Government intervention as acceptable when it gives (e.g., Government supported developments such as aircraft), and wrong when it demands (especially in the field of information).

(d) We must be vigilant to assert that personal choice is one of the mainsprings of human endeavours, and that restrictionist intervention, by denying choice saps initiative and so economic growth.

(e) Finally, in cases where we are not clear about the ends, and accept the means, or even in cases where we are not clear but Parliament has ordained, we must co-operate in a real sense of partnership.[17]

Although the Royal Navy might appear to be one of the 'parastatal' bodies criticised by Rowan, its relationship with the Wireless Telegraph and Signal Company conformed largely with these five criteria.[18] Its activities, both as regards wireless telegraphy and in the wider context of the Fleet's expansion during the 1890s had all been approved by Parliament; it took part in an unrestricted exchange of information and ideas with the civilian manufacturer; both parties were free to enter into similar relationships elsewhere if it seemed advantageous.

Government sponsorship, and especially sponsorship from one of the armed services, was particularly valuable to Marconi's company in its very early days when investments and profits were small. Cost, so far as the Royal Navy was concerned, was not a major problem. Their real need was for apparatus that would provide high performance during relatively short periods of time; low performance at a lower price was a false economy for military equipment, as a few expensive warships of the best possible quality could easily destroy a much larger fleet of cheaper vessels in battle.[19] In any case, a Marconi radio set costing about two hundred pounds, with a further one hundred pounds a year royalty, was a negligible addition to the cost of a contemporary battleship at about a million pounds – or even of a small scouting cruiser costing a quarter of a million.

Radio was not 'big business' in the early years of the twentieth century. Its market was the very limited one provided by the world's navies, and its manufacturing needs were little more than those of a home workshop or a rural garage. The expansion of this market came only gradually before the First World War, with radio being adopted for merchant ships – especially after favourable publicity for radio as an element in the rescue of passengers from the wrecked liners *Florida* in 1909 and *Titanic* in 1912. The outbreak of war in 1914 brought an increased demand for military communications equipment, as well as an increase in the numbers of radio technicians trained by the armed services in most industrial countries. But the real growth of business occurred in the decade after the war. By the 1920s, technological advances meant that radio could at last compete for some of the international traffic until then carried exclusively by the submarine cables. Even more significantly, the development of radio broadcasting as a medium of information and entertainment meant that every family in the world had become a potential customer for radio sets. This was 'big business' with a mass market at last, the sort of business in which the large electrical combines such as AEG and Siemens-Schuckert in Germany or General Electric in the USA were organised to operate most effectively. Their radio subsidiaries – Telefunken and the Radio Corporation of America – flourished, often at the expense of Marconi.

It was in the period before the First World War, when the main market for radio sets came from naval communications orders, that Britain, through the Marconi organisation, dominated the world's industry. Radio was then, very definitely, an 'advanced technology' and the State's investment in this technology, as represented by the original naval contract with Marconi's, was quite large by British standards at the time. Table 13.1 compares the value of this contract with the much-publicised investment of public money in the National Physical Laboratory at about the same period.

With this level of support from the Royal Navy, the Marconi organisation came to resemble the various armaments contractors who were also dependent on naval orders for their income. Marder has observed that

British armament firms, like their continental rivals, never hesitated to arm other countries, even enemies, if there was a great profit to be made. Foreign

Table 13.1 *Government investment in the NPL, 1898, and in radio telegraphy for the Royal Navy, 1900*

	Initial grant	Annual budget
National Physical Laboratory	£12,000	£4,000

	Purchase price	Annual royalty
Marconi contract (radio sets)	£6,000	£3,200

Sources: Randman, *Government Science*, p. 78; Chapter 12 of this book.

sales increased profits in another way. The more armaments were increased abroad, especially in enemy countries, the more they had to be increased at home. More extraordinary were the international rings formed to intensify the arms rivalry by the exchange of patents and secrets and to maintain high prices. Another practice of the armament magnates was their eagerness to avail themselves of the services of responsible officials of the Admiralty and War Office, for the knowledge and 'contacts' possessed by these men were of great use to them.[20]

Marconi, Jameson Davis and Flood Page could in no way have been described as 'magnates' during the late nineteenth and early twentieth centuries. But there were then already indications that their Company's policies were acquiring the characteristics which Marder has described. Marconi organised demonstrations of radio for the French and United States' navies in 1899, during the months after the Fashoda confrontation, when anti-British feeling in France was at its height and the attitude of the United States was one of cautious neutrality. Yet the British officers associated with Marconi regarded such foreign negotiations as legitimate business, and even remarked that 'they would show rather a reason for having the system in the service, than not, if only for the purpose of incommoding our possible enemies'.[21] The cultivation of useful contacts within the Royal Navy had started as early as August 1896, when Marconi met Jackson at the War Office. There is no example of an international ring to control radio trade during the period of this study – radio telegraphy was too much in its infancy – but the Marconi organisation did conclude such an agreement with their principal commercial rivals, Telefunken, a few years later.

By the end of the nineteenth century, therefore, the radio industry in Britain was no longer a small isolated company. It was becoming, in a primitive form, a prototype for the kind of military-industrial complex based on an advanced technology that would be familiar later in the twentieth century. The success of the Marconi group, identified as an exception to the general pattern of British industrial decline which Wiener and others have discussed, is no longer seen as exceptional when this group is considered as part of the country's naval armaments industry. For, as Kirby points out:

Britain did manage to retain an impressive international lead down to 1914 in a number of industries [including] ... the armaments sector of heavy industry and shipbuilding ... Studies ... of the production and marketing record of industries such as these have gone a considerable way towards undermining the blanket hypothesis of entrepreneurial failure.[22]

The fortunes of those industries which supplied the needs of Imperial communications and Imperial defence stood in conspicuous contrast to the less-successful British enterprises dependent largely on commercial markets. Some of the Imperial communications industries, like the submarine cable companies, had evolved monopolistic structures that were tolerated by the same government who would not permit the development of monopoly in other enterprises. Others, such as the warship builders, were favoured by government policies that ensured most of their capacity would be occupied with large lucrative orders. Their personnel came from the one sector of British society which was provided with an adequate system of higher technical education, whether through the military schools of science, the specialised apprentice schools or through the State-supported technical colleges. And it was not only the manufacturers who benefitted from this State education system; their customers, too, had studied applied science at the State's expense. The leaders of the Royal Navy in the early twentieth century, including Fisher, Jellicoe, Jackson and even King George V himself, all were educated in the Royal Naval College at Greenwich and in HMS *Vernon*.

The radio industry was but a small part of this sector providing the Empire's communications and defence requirements, but it shared in that sector's general prosperity. Although there was no large electrical manufacturer in Britain to provide the financial backing enjoyed by Marconi's rivals in Germany, the government, through the Royal Navy, made up for the deficiency. While British investment in scientific education was generally less than that in other major industrial countries, the government-supported technical colleges and University of London were enough to meet the needs of the small radio industry (even Rutherford, the only leading Cambridge physicist to carry out any practical radio research, received a State-financed education with an Exhibition Fellowship). For so long as radio was regarded primarily as a means of communication between warships, the Marconi organisation had exclusive access to the largest available market in the world – and this market, too, was government-controlled. No foreign radio company received State support on such a scale. Britain's radio industry rapidly achieved world dominance, and it retained its dominant place for the whole of the period in which the industry's output was devoted entirely to meeting the State's communications needs, and so protecting the Empire's interests.

References

1   *The Times*, 8 September 1888.

2   G.F. Fitzgerald, *The Electrician*, XXXI, 1893, p.389.

3   E.E. Fournier d'Alba, *Life of Sir William Crookes*, London, Fisher Unwin, 1923, p.3.

4   J.J. O'Neill, *Prodigal Genius: the Life of Nikola Tesla*, London, Neville Spearman, 1968, p.252.

5   O.J. Lodge, *Advancing Science*, London, Benn, 1931, p.337.

6   B.L. Jacot and D.M.B. Collier, *Marconi, Master of Space*, London, Hutchinson, 1935, pp.218–19.

7   G.F.C. Searle, 'Oliver Heaviside – a personal sketch', *The Heaviside Centenary Volume*, London, The Institution of Electrical Engineers, 1950, p.95.

8   *The Times*, 23 September 1896.

9   Oliver Heaviside had worked as a telegrapher, but resigned from his post more than ten years before the period of this study. Lodge was to be employed as a consultant by the telegraph industry several years later. Neither was associated with telegraph engineering during the early years of radio development.

10   R.A.S. Hennessey, *The Electric Revolution*, Stocksfield, Oriel Press, 1972, pp.4, 5, 157–8.

11   W.P. Jolly, *Sir Oliver Lodge, Psychical Researcher and Scientist*, London, Constable, 1974, pp.51–2.

12   A.J. Marder, *The Anatomy of British Sea Power: A History of British Naval Policy in the Pre-Dreadnought Era, 1880–1905*, London, Frank Cass & Co., 1964, pp.35, 175–205.

13   J. Ruskin, *The Crown of Wild Olive*, London, George Allen [1865] 1906, p.123.

14   G.R. White and M.B.W. Graham, 'How to spot a technological winner', *Harvard Business Review*, LVI, 1978, pp.146–52.

15   'Annual Report of the Torpedo School (HMS *Vernon*)' for 1901, p.111 (NHL).

16   A. Hezlet, *The Electron and Sea Power*, London, Peter Davies, 1975, p. 38; G. E. Weir, *The Origins of German Seapower: Military-Industrial Relationships in the Development of the High Seas Fleet, 1897–1912*, PhD Dissertation, University of Tennessee, 1982.

17   H. Evans, *Vickers: Against the Odds*, London, Hodder & Stoughton, 1978, pp. 40–2.

18   Sir Leslie Rowan (1908–72) resigned as Second Secretary of the Treasury to join Vickers Ltd in 1958. He was the company's Chairman in 1967, when he defined the above criteria during an address at the London Graduate School of Business Studies. Sir Leslie was therefore speaking from experience in senior posts on both the government and the commercial sides of State-supported industries.

19   This distinction between military and civilian needs has not always been appreciated by British industry. To cite three examples since the Second World War – Vickers suffered heavy losses in 1960 in an attempt to convert a tank production line to manufacturing agricultural tractors; success with the Magnox reactor originally intended to produce military plutonium misled the CEGB into drastic under-estimates of time and cost for the civil advanced gas-cooled reactor in 1965; Rolls-Royce, after a profitable series of military gas turbines, were bankrupted by the civil RB 211 aero engine in 1971.

20   P. Randman, *Government Science in Britain, 1875–1921*, MSc Thesis, University of Manchester, 1977, p. 78.

21   Marder, *British Sea Power*, pp. 26–7.

22   Commander Evan-Thomas to the President of the Signal Committee, 10 May 1898 (PRO, file ADM 116/523).

23   M. W. Kirby, *The Decline of British Economic Power since 1870*, London, Allen & Unwin, 1981, p. 9.

Bibliography

(a) Manuscripts and reports with limited circulation

Institution of Electrical Engineers, Savoy Place, London WC2R 0BL

    W. H. Preece papers, file Sc Ms 22

    A. E. Trotter, *Reminiscences* (in four bound volumes of manuscript)

National Army Museum, Royal Hospital Road, London SW3 4HT

    Royal Engineers' Committee Minute Books for 1896 and 1897

National Maritime Museum, Greenwich, London SE10 9NF

    R. Bayly, *Electrical Communication on the Coasts of the United Kingdom*, Plymouth Chamber of Commerce, 1892 (Pamphlet collection, No P 262)

Naval Historical Library, Empress State Building, London SW6 1 TR

    Annual Reports of the Torpedo School (HMS *Vernon*), 1887 to 1901

    Extracts from the Report of the Committee on the Naval Manoeuvres, 1888

    Parliamentary Returns: Fleets, Great Britain and Foreign Countries, 1888

    Report of the Committee Appointed by the Admiralty to Inquire into the System of Training Naval Cadets on Board HMS *Britannia*, 1875

    Report of the Committee Appointed to Inquire into the Establishment of the Royal Naval College, Greenwich, 1877

    Report of the Committee on the Higher Education of Naval Officers, 1870

    The Navy List, 1887

Post Office Records, St Martins le Grand, London EC1A 1PG

    Files: Eng 23109/1899
           Eng 26173/1903
           Eng 26411/1903

Public Record Office, Chancery Lane, London WC2A 1LR

    Files: ADM 116/523
           ADM 116/534
           ADM 116/567
           ADM 116/570
              WO 32/989, file 84/M/3975
                      file 84/M/4009

The Marconi Company Limited, Victoria Road, Chelmsford CM1 1NY
    Files: HIS 43
            HIS 62
            HIS 63
            HIS 64
The typewritten 'de Sousa' manuscript
Typewritten copy of G. S. Kemp's diary for 1897 to 1899

(b) Printed sources

Aitken, H. G. J.   *Syntony and Spark — the Origins of Radio*, New York: John Wiley, 1976

Appleyard, R.   *The History of the Institution of Electrical Engineers, 1871–1931*, London: IEE, 1939

Archer, G. L.   *History of Radio to 1926*, New York: American Historical Society, 1938

Baker, E. C.   *Sir William Preece, FRS: Victorian Engineer Extraordinary*, London: Hutchinson, 1976

Baker, W. J.   *A History of the Marconi Company*, London: Methuen, 1970

Barnett, C.   (1979) 'Technology, education and industrial and economic strength', *Journal of the Royal Society of Arts*, 127: 118–27

Cardwell, D. S. L.   *The Organisation of Science in England*, London: Heinemann, 1972

Chalmers, A. F.   (1971) *The Electromagnetic Theory of James Clerk Maxwell*, PhD Thesis, University of London

DeKosky, R. K.   (1976) 'William Crookes and the Fourth State of Matter', *Isis*, 67:36–60

Eastwood, E.   (1974) 'Marconi, pioneer of wireless telegraphy', *Electronics and Power*, 20:308–11

Erskine-Murray, J.   [1907] *A Handbook of Wireless Telegraphy*, London: Crosby Lockwood & Son, 1913

Evans, H.   *Vickers: Against the Odds*, London: Hodder & Stoughton, 1978

Fahie, J. J.   *A History of Wireless Telegraphy*, Edinburgh: Blackwood, 1899

Fleming, J. A.   *Principles of Electric Wave Telegraphy*, London: Longmans, 1906

Fournier d'Albe, E. E. *Life of Sir William Crookes*, London: Fisher Unwin, 1923

Frith, H. and Rawson, W. S.   *Coil and Current, or the Triumphs of Electricity*, London: Ward Lock, [1896]

Garcke, E.   'Telegraphy', *Encyclopaedia Britannica*, 11th edition, 1911

Garratt, G.R.M.   *One Hundred Years of Submarine Cables*, London: The Science Museum, 1950

Geddes, K.   *Guglielmo Marconi: 1874–1937*, London: The Science Museum, 1974

Geddes, K.   (1975) 'The GPO and the Telephone, 1877–1879', *Papers Presented at the Third IEE Weekend Meeting on the History of Electrical Engineering*, 11/1 – 11/9

Ghemawat, P.   (1985) 'Building strategy on the experience curve', *Harvard Business Review*, 64:143–9

Goetzeler, H.   (1975) 'Ferdinand Braun and die Drahtlosen Tele-graphia an der Nordsee', *Deutsches Schiffahrtsarchiv*, 5:151–8

Halsey, R.J.   (1968) 'Britain's contribution to telecommunications', *Electronics and Power*, 14:354–7

Heaviside, O.   *Electrical Papers*, London: Macmillan, 1892

Hennessey, R.A.S.   *The Electric Revolution*, Stocksfield, Northumberland: Oriel Press, 1972

Hertz, H.   *Untersuchungen über die Ausbreitung der elektrischen Kraft*, Leipzig: Johann Ambrosius Barth, 1892

Hertz, H.   *Electric Waves* (English translation of the above by D.E. Jones), London: Macmillan, 1893

Hezlet, A.   *The Electron and Sea Power*, London: Peter Davies, 1975

Hobsbawm, E.J.   *Industry and Empire* (Volume 3 of The Pelican Economic History of Britain), Harmondsworth: Penguin, 1969

Hunt, B.J.   (1983) 'Practice vs theory: the British electrical debate, 1888–1891', *Isis* 74:341–55

Jackson, W.   'An appreciation of Heaviside's contribution to electro-magnetic theory', in *The Heaviside Centenary Volume*, London: The Institution of Electrical Engineers, 1950

Jacot, B.L. and   *Marconi, Master of Space*, London: Hutchinson,
Collier, D.M.B.   1935

Jolly, W.P.   *Marconi*, London: Constable, 1972

Jolly, W.P.   *Sir Oliver Lodge, Psychical Researcher and Scientist*, London: Constable, 1974

Kieve, J.L.   *The Electric Telegraph: a Social and Economic History*, Newton Abbot: David & Charles, 1973

Kirby, M.W.   *The Decline of British Economic Power since 1870*, London: Allen & Unwin, 1981

Landes, D.S.   [1969] *The Unbound Prometheus*, Cambridge: Cambridge University Press, 1980

Lee, G.   'Oliver Heaviside, the man', in *The Heaviside Centenary Volume*, London: The Institution of Electrical Engineers, 1950.

Lodge, O.J.   *The Work of Hertz and His Successors*, London: The Electrician Printing & Publishing Co., 1894

Lodge, O.J.   *Past Years*, London: Hodder & Stoughton, 1931 (a)

Lodge, O.J.   *Advancing Science*, London: Benn, 1931 (b)

Logan, K.D.   (1976) *The Admiralty: Reforms and Reorganisation, 1868–1892*, PhD Thesis, University of Oxford

Macleod, R.M.   (1969) 'Science and government in Victorian England: lighthouse illumination and the Board of Trade, 1866–1886', *Isis*, 60:5–38

Macleod, R.M.   (1971) 'The support of Victorian science: the endowment of research movement in Great Britain', *Minerva* 9:197–230

Marder, A.J.   *From the Dreadnought to Scapa Flow*, Oxford: Oxford University Press, 1961

Marder, A.J.   [1940] *The Anatomy of British Sea Power: A History of British Naval Policy in the Pre-Dreadnought Era, 1880–1905*, London: Frank Cass & Co., 1964

Marx, K. and   [1888] *The Communist Manifesto* (English translation
Engels, F.   from the original German text of 1848), Harmondsworth: Penguin, 1978

Muirhead, M.E.   *Alexander Muirhead*, published privately, Oxford, 1926

O'Neill, J.J.   *Prodigal Genius: the Life of Nikola Tesla*, London: Neville Spearman, 1968

Paresce-Marconi, D. *My Father Marconi*, Wimbledon: Muller, 1962

Passer, H.C.   *The Electrical Manufacturers, 1875–1900*, Cambridge, Mass.: Harvard University Press, 1953

Pieper, H.   (1975) 'Die englischen Bemühungen vor dem Ersten Weltkrieg um ein weltweites Kabel- und Funkmonopol', *Archiv für deutsche Postgeschichte*, 1:79–95

Pocock, R.F. and   *The Origins of Maritime Radio*, London: The Science
Garratt, G.R.M.   Museum, 1972

Preece, W.H. and   [1874] *Telegraphy*, London: Longmans Green, 1891
Sivewright, J.

Randman, P.   (1977) *Government Science in Britain, 1875–1921*, M Sc Thesis, University of Manchester

Ruskin, J.   [1865] *The Crown of Wild Olive*, London: George Allen, 1906

Sayer, G.B.	*HMS Vernon: a History*, Portsmouth: Ward Room Mess Committee, HMS *Vernon*, 1930
Searle, G.F.C.	'Oliver Heaviside – a personal sketch', in *The Heaviside Centenary Volume*, London: The Institution of Electrical Engineers, 1950
Sharlin, H.I.	*The Making of the Electrical Age*, New York: Abelard-Schuman, 1963
Smith, C.A.	(1977) 'The corrosion story', *Anti-Corrosion*, 24:12–15
Sturmey, S.G.	*The Economic Development of Radio*, London: Duckworth, 1958
Süsskind, C.	(1962) 'Popov and the beginnings of radiotelegraphy, *Proceedings of the Institute of Radio Engineers*, 50: 2036–47
Süsskind, C.	(1964) 'Observations of electromagnetic wave radiation before Hertz', *Isis*, 55:32–42
Süsskind, C.	'The early history of electronics', *Institute of Electrical and Electronics Engineers Spectrum*, 5:90–8 (Aug. 1968) and 57–60 (Dec. 1968), 6:69–74 (Apr. 1969) and 66–70 (Aug. 1969), 7:78–83 (Apr. 1970) and 76–9 (Sept. 1970)
Trebilcock, C.	*The Industrialization of the Continental Powers*, London: Longman, 1981
Tucker D.G.	(1982) 'Sir William Preece (1834–1913)', *Transactions of the Newcomen Society*, 53:119–38
Vvedensky, B.	'Popov, A.S.', *The Great Soviet Encyclopaedia* (English translation), 1955
Watts, P.	'Ship', *Encyclopaedia Britannica*, 11th edition, 1911
Weir, G.E.	(1982) *The Origins of German Seapower: Military-Industrial Relationships in the Development of the High Seas Fleet, 1897–1912*, PhD Dissertation, University of Tennessee
White, G.R. and Graham, M.B.W.	(1978) 'How to spot a technological winner', *Harvard Business Review*, 56:146–52
Whittaker, E.	'Address at the Heaviside Centenary Meeting', in *The Heaviside Centenary Volume*, London: The Institution of Electrical Engineers, 1950
Wiener, M.J.	*English Culture and the Decline of the Industrial Spirit*, Cambridge: Cambridge University Press, 1981
Wilson, D.	*Rutherford, Simple Genius*, London: Hodder & Stoughton, 1983

Index